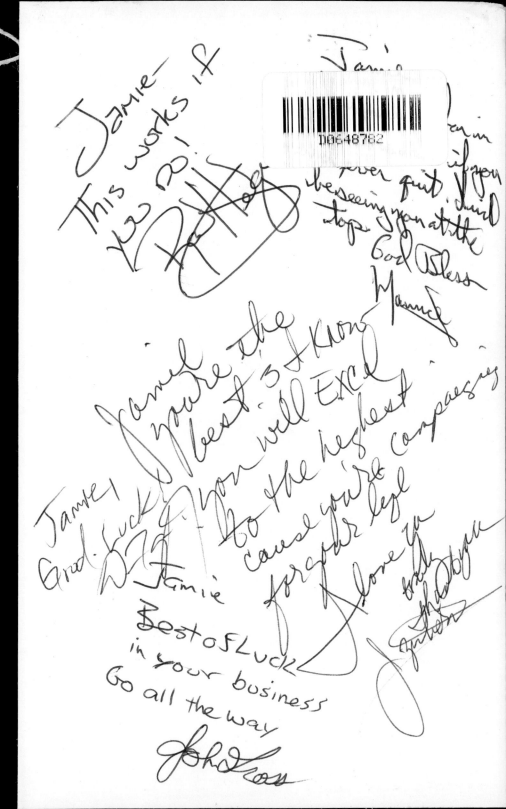

Jamie—
This works if
You Do!
[signature]

Jamie
[...] am in
[...] never quit. I will
be seeing you at the
top. God Bless

Jamie
you're the
best. & I know
Grad. Luck you will Excel
to the highest
cause you're compassing
for your legl
I love you
[signature]

Jamie
Best of Luck
in your business
Go all the way
John Cross

THE EXCEL PHENOMENON

James W. Robinson

FOREWORD BY **Kenny A. Troutt**
CHAIRMAN AND CHIEF EXECUTIVE OFFICER,
EXCEL COMMUNICATIONS, INC.

PHENOMENON

The Astonishing Success Story

of the Fastest-Growing

Communications Company—

and What It Means to You

PRIMA PUBLISHING

PRIMA PUBLISHING and colophon are trademarks of Prima Communications, Inc.

Library of Congress Cataloging-in-Publication Data

Robinson, James W.
    The Excel phenomenon: the astonishing success story of the fastest-growing telecommunications company—and what it means to you / James W. Robinson.
        p.   cm.
    Includes index.
    ISBN 0-7615-1171-7
    1. Excel Communications.   2. Telephone—United States—Long distance.   3. Telecommunication—United States.   I. Title.
HE8846.E95R63 1997
384'.06'573—dc21   97-23828
                                                                     CIP

97 98 99 00 HH 10 9 8 7 6 5 4 3
Printed in the United States of America

How to Order
Single copies may be ordered from Prima Publishing, P.O. Box 1260BK, Rocklin, CA 95677; telephone (916) 632-4400. Quantity discounts are also available. On your letterhead, include information concerning the intended use of the books and the number of books you wish to purchase.

Visit us online at http://www.primapublishing.com

Contents

Foreword by Kenny A. Troutt   vii

Preface   xi

Acknowledgments   xix

Note to the Reader   xxiii

ONE: A Winning Combination   1

TWO: Ringing the Bell   25

THREE: "The Most Impressive Thing
I've Ever Seen"   49

FOUR: Answering the Question Why   71

FIVE: Independence Day   91

SIX: Remembering What's Important   115

SEVEN: It's Not Too Late   135

EIGHT: No More Excuses   159

NINE: Imagine!   185

TEN: An Interview with Kenny Troutt   209

Conclusion: Ten Questions for Your Future   217

Index   221

Foreword

WHEN I BEGAN Excel Communications in 1988, I had a lot of dreams and expectations for the new company. But I never dreamed or expected that less than 10 years after we started there would be a whole book written about the changes we are bringing to the telecommunications business and the positive impact we are making on people's lives.

Because Excel has traveled so far so fast in such a high-profile industry, our company has received a great deal of attention in the nation's leading business publications. As the company's founder, I've been quoted in the press frequently as well. But a big part of our story has not been told—until now. It concerns the people in our business who have seen the vision, grabbed hold of the opportunity we offered them, and achieved great things for themselves and their families through free enterprise. Jim Robinson brings many of Excel's leading Independent Representatives to life in *The Excel Phenomenon,* and I am pleased and very proud that they are getting the recognition they deserve.

Excel has fundamentally changed both the telecommunications industry and the network marketing business in our country. We plan to continue to lead this change in the years ahead. Jim has clearly articulated both our achievements and our vision for the future.

More important, when you read this book, you can come away with a powerful feeling of excitement and optimism about the times in which we live.

We face serious problems, to be sure. Many Americans are rightfully concerned about their financial security. They lack confidence in the ability of both big business and big government to continue to provide either a rewarding career or an adequate social safety net. They are deeply troubled by the lack of time and attention they are able to give to their children, due to the time demands of the modern-day workplace. Too many have deferred their most cherished dreams for too long.

All of this can be changed. None of it need be accepted. That's the vital message of *The Excel Phenomenon*. Whether you choose to participate in our business or another, this book offers a compelling case that it has never been easier to start your own business and strike out on your own. The opportunities have never been greater for you to become your own boss, build a business with your family by your side, and take control of your time, your life, and your dreams once again.

I'm very proud of the role Excel has played in fostering a new era of promise and excitement for American entrepreneurs. What we have tried to do is create a business opportunity that is open and accessible to all, that strengthens the family, and that embraces the principle that you can best achieve your financial goals and personal aspirations by helping others achieve theirs. This book tells you how we did it and how you can become part of our vision.

And Jim is exactly right when he says that the only suitable ending for *The Excel Phenomenon* is one that's expressed by the words "To be continued . . ." Because whether you're from Wall Street or Main Street, I can promise you this—you ain't seen nothing yet!

Kenny A. Troutt
Chairman and Chief Executive Officer
Excel Communications, Inc.

THIS IS THE story of a remarkable business opportunity that is open to all and is as simple to understand as using the telephone. The company calls itself Excel Communications. I call it the Excel Phenomenon. Founded in 1988 by entrepreneur Kenny A. Troutt, Excel entered the telecommunications industry as a regional reseller of long-distance telephone service in the aftermath of the breakup of AT&T. It is now a major national player, having gathered some four million customers in a fiercely competitive business without spending a dime on TV ads or Hollywood celebrities. It has become a billion-dollar-plus company almost faster than any new company in American history.

Excel did it by purchasing blocks of long-distance service at deep discounts and then enlisting hundreds of thousands of Independent Representatives to resell that service to members of their families, friends, and business associates in a network marketing system. In the process, many of these Independent Representatives have built their own businesses and enhanced their financial security by earning commissions from the long-distance calls of the customers they sign up as well as from the calls of their recruits' recruits.

Few would question that Excel is an interesting business story. But why write a book about a long-distance reseller that commands only about 3 percent of just one piece of a global telecommunications industry that will surpass $1 *trillion* in worldwide revenues shortly after the turn of the century? My answer is that Excel represents something much larger than itself. It is the embodiment of some of the most powerful socioeconomic and cultural trends in America today:

o The reaffirmation of the role of individual initiative in the economic life of the country
o The creation of an entrepreneurship that makes room for, and strengthens, the American family
o The development of a new business value system based on the idea that capitalism works best with an ethic not of "dog eat dog" but rather of "people helping people"

The story of Excel should be told, not because this company is growing faster or making money more quickly than other companies but because it is changing people's lives in positive ways that both big government and big businesses have tried and failed to do.

Excel accomplishes this because its leaders have had the vision to ideally position their company at the center of the following events:

o A global revolution in the demand for telecommunications services and technologies

o The steady evolution of American business toward
the powerful concepts of network marketing

o The transformation of network marketing itself,
from a product-based industry to a service-based
industry

The emergence of Excel also vividly illustrates how
the unleashing of free market principles in a key industry
can trigger a chain reaction of positive developments
that extend far beyond that industry. Old assumptions
are challenged. New ideas are introduced. Mind-sets are
changed.

Think about it. For nearly a century, there was basically one phone company that enjoyed monopolistic
power in the marketplace. Almost everyone—scholars
and economists, politicians and presidents, giant
commercial customers and the individual consumer—
simply assumed that's the way it had to be and would
always remain.

Then, in the early 1980s, the breakup of that
monopoly and the momentum created by it opened an
opportunity for a young entrepreneur. Kenny Troutt,
who grew up in the housing projects of East St. Louis
and who knew nothing about telecommunications, was
able to start a long-distance phone company without
installing a single switch or laying a foot of fiber into
the ground.

In less than 10 years, he and his partners grew that upstart company into the fifth-largest residential long distance provider in the nation. In the process, they created an opportunity for tens of thousands of others to start their own home-based businesses with an investment of a couple hundred dollars. Some have become multimillionaires in the process. Many others have achieved varying measures of financial independence and security.

Please understand that *The Excel Phenomenon* must be a story with a "To be continued . . ." ending. One leading Excel Representative told me, "Jim, you're writing the first book about Excel, but there's going to be many more books written before we're through!" I believe him.

When I started work on this book, the company had just announced, with considerable fanfare, that it was beginning a gradual migration from being a switchless reseller of long-distance service to a company that would back up that approach with the installation of its own network. The effort was to begin with the purchase of six state-of-the-art switches. Several months later, I heard Kenny Troutt announce that the first three switches were going to be installed in New York, Dallas, and Los Angeles.

Then, just as I was completing my work, a dramatic new development was announced that shook the telecommunications world: Excel declared that it would acquire Telco Communications Group, one of the nation's 10 largest long-distance phone companies, with its own network that includes $1 billion in installed equipment. The deal would transform Excel overnight into a $2 billion company.

I have to admit, I didn't even see it coming! That's how fast the telecommunications business is changing and that's how fast this company is embracing change and new ideas. Steve Smith, Excel's executive vice president of marketing and the architect of its network marketing plan, told a group of Representatives recently that they wouldn't recognize the company in a few months. I figured he was merely engaging in a little razzle-dazzle rhetoric to fire up the troops. Now we all know better.

In tracing the footsteps of Excel from infancy to today, one can, of course, find false starts and mistakes along the way. But for those who dream of the possibilities that can come from challenging the conventional wisdom and for those who need reassurance that ideas still count in our society, the story of Excel will intrigue you as much as it did me.

From a personal perspective, chronicling the achievements of Kenny Troutt, Steve Smith, Jack McLaine, and dozens of top Excel Representatives has sparked a reexamination of my own life and career.

For nearly 20 years, I have experienced many opportunities to meet, observe, and work for some of the greatest leaders in American business and politics. I drafted radio and newspaper commentaries for Ronald Reagan and served as a senior aide to a California governor and a U.S. Congressman. I have flown around the country in the corporate jets of senior business executives, advising them on communications strategies and writing their speeches. My international trade work on behalf of the state of California created memorable experiences, such as participating in small meetings with world leaders such as Britain's Margaret Thatcher, Mikhail Gorbachev of the former Soviet Union, and Corazon Aquino of the Philippines.

Moreover, my previous books on business communications, commercial opportunities in Vietnam, the political phenomena of Ross Perot and the Republican Congress elected in 1994, and the pioneering network marketing company, Amway, have afforded me close-up exposure to a broad spectrum of watershed developments in business and public policy.

It has been a career filled with excitement and challenge, one that has earned me a more-than-comfortable income. But something has always been missing. By focusing on helping others, through communications, to project *their* leadership, build *their* financial or political fortunes, and advance *their* ideas, I have neglected my own aspirations. Why? Because it's easy to get caught up in the trappings and status of the rich and powerful— and it's safer to stand in the long shadows cast by others than it is to step into the glare and cast your own.

Seven years ago, as George Deukmejian was winding up eight years as California's governor, I was preparing to leave my politically appointed post as well. Rather than seek another government post, I decided to branch out on my own. Having been so close to the center of power in California, I considered anything else to be a serious letdown. Besides, I reasoned that I could easily translate the contacts I had made into a lucrative consulting and lobbying business. On a more serious note, I felt that continuing to derive my livelihood from a government job while vigorously espousing the virtues of free enterprise and limited government was a complexity soon to blossom into a contradiction.

Governor Deukmejian put it more plainly. "It's time to put your money where your mouth is," he said. So I did—and I flopped! Not so much financially, for I was at least able to generate enough consulting and freelance writing activity to pay the bills. But I realized how little I knew about how to build my own business. I was insecure and feared rejection so much that I deliberately made my pitch calls to prospective clients at lunchtime and other inopportune times of the day, in the hope that I would miss them and get their voice mail recording instead!

I lacked the discipline to work productively at home, where there are dozens of excuses and distractions to pull you away from your desk. Perhaps most of all, I missed the status and identity that came from serving in high office. It's awful to be known as a "former." I was ashamed.

Within nine months, I beat a hasty retreat back to a government office and took a job with less pay and stature than the one I had previously left. Since then, I have held several interesting jobs. I'm safe and secure in the high-flying, pressure-filled world of political communications. I've got a fancy office again with a high salary and a 70-hour work week. I have wonderful colleagues who implement my instructions, make my travel arrangements, and manage my schedule. I'm a player.

However, there's still something missing. I still haven't proved I can stand on my own. I still haven't demonstrated I can practice what I preach. I'm still not in control of my own life. I'm still standing in the shadows.

For the last six months, I have been given a rare chance to meet a group of people who have achieved those things that have proved so elusive to me—and perhaps to you as well. Going backstage at Excel and tracing its leaders' journeys from the shadows to the limelight has emboldened me to prepare for another such journey of my own. This time, I think I'll know where I'm going and how to get there.

Getting to know the people of Excel has brought me ever closer to my own personal day of reckoning. For that, I thank them—especially the more than two dozen Representatives who tried to sign me up! I'm not there yet, but I will be soon. By the time you finish reading *The Excel Phenomenon,* you may be, too.

Whether you conclude that this is the right business for you or you find another opportunity to join the millions of Americans setting out on their own, my goal is to help you see that the choice and the power to change your life is in your hands and yours alone.

Acknowledgments

NETWORK MARKETERS LIKE to say that in their industry you may be in business *for* yourself, but you are not in business *by* yourself. We only succeed if we have the support and encouragement of people who trust and believe in us.

The same holds true when writing a book. Of course there are endless days and nights in solitude with the door slammed shut, the television off, the coffeepot on, phone messages unanswered, back aching, head pounding, deadlines looming, and one's temper snapping. But what keeps us going is the sustenance we draw from the people around us. *The Excel Phenomenon* may have been a book written by one person, but it is not a book that was written alone.

Kevin Ganster is a tremendously talented writer, researcher, and editor whose contributions to the book cannot be overstated.

The team at Prima Publishing—including Susan Silva, Kathy Daniel, Scott Pink, Karen Blanco, and Steven Martin—is first-class and professional all the way. Working with them is always a rewarding experience.

Tom Donohue continues to spur me on with his own endless energy and drive for excellence. Dick Lesher, winding up nearly a quarter of a century of outstanding leadership as U.S. Chamber of Commerce president, always inspires me with his passion for America and the free enterprise system.

My conclusions about Excel are independently drawn. I am not part of the Excel business and derive no compensation from the company.

Yet the people of Excel, starting with Kenny Troutt and Steve Smith and carrying right on through to the Presidential Directors and Senior Directors, Eagle Team members, and many others, have provided a level of cooperation and assistance a writer can only dream of. You are too many to mention here, but I am grateful to each of you.

Excel's Sharon Holman deserves a very special thank you. Relatively new at her job when I started bombarding her with requests and questions, she was never too busy to help. Her support encouraged me greatly every step of the way. The same goes for Gabrielle Farina, whom I cannot thank enough for her tireless efforts.

Two others must be mentioned.

Ben Dominitz, who with his wife, Nancy, started Prima in the family garage and built it into the innovative publishing powerhouse it is today, is one of the most visionary and compassionate individuals I have ever met. The idea to write *The Excel Phenomenon* began with Ben, and that's something everyone should know.

Ben has published all of my work to date, and I am grateful to him for enabling me to achieve the part of my identity that I like best. But even if he had never published a word, I would still feel greatly privileged to be his friend.

The Vietnamese have a proverb that, loosely translated into English, says: "Even though the tree tries to stay steady, there are winds blowing all around it." As the winds have blown all around him, my friend, Duc Huu Nguyen, has remained steady as the strongest tree in the forest.

Two decades ago, he fled a failed war and a ravaged homeland. Beginning anew in this country as a dishwasher, he helped two dozen family members flee oppression and build new lives here. He never went to college because he was working too hard to ensure that the next generation of his family could.

In the face of so many challenges, Duc's quiet courage has set a strong example for me. I thank him for all he has done for me and for the outstanding example he has set for others.

Note to the Reader

WHEN I BEGAN the process of researching and writing *The Excel Phenomenon*, I had only a sketchy knowledge of Excel as a company and no set opinions about it. Readers will surely note that I have since come to the conclusion that, on the whole, Excel is having a significant and positive impact on telecommunications, network marketing, and on the lives of many of the people who have joined the business.

While I have received an unprecedented level of access from Excel, my opinions and conclusions are my own. This book has been independently published by Prima, a major U.S. publishing house. I am not part of Excel and receive no compensation from the company.

In this day and age, it's easy to find things that don't work. I hope you'll agree with me that it's kind of refreshing to find and write about something that does.

James W. Robinson

A WINNING COMBINATION

FRIDAY, MAY 16, 7:00 P.M. It's hazy and warm in Los Angeles. In a cavernous auditorium of the L.A. Convention Center, 1,500 people have gathered, having fought through the rush-hour traffic and shaken off the end-of-the-week exhaustion. For those coming directly from their nine-to-five jobs, there has been no time for dinner. That will have to wait.

I try to form some generalizations about the people in the crowd, but I can't. The only thing they have in common with one another is that they're different from one another. Young people and old people, families and single people, men and women, suits and blue jeans, silks and polyester, fitness buffs and the wheelchair-bound—

here is an ethnic and racial melting pot as diverse as Los Angeles itself.

Pulsating dance music, complete with lights and lasers, jolts the crowd to attention. The hall darkens, the stage lights up, and the crowd rises in unison and lets out a lusty cheer. While much of America is complacently absorbed in thank-God-it's-Friday pursuits, these people are energized and motivated. They have come in search of something new and different, and their journey is about to begin.

A young man named Steve Schulz takes the stage. One of the most successful of Excel's Independent Representatives, he begins by telling the audience of the day that he and his boyhood friend and business partner Pat Hintze got their first commission check from the company seven years ago. With their wives by their sides, they excitedly tore open the envelope and looked at the grand total: a check for 46 cents ("And don't forget, we had to split it two ways!").

Steve didn't care: "All I needed was that first check to tell me that the system was in place. It worked." In response to Steve's story, an explosion of cheers rocks the hall.

How does it work? With the aid of diagrams flashed on a big screen, Steve boils it down to the simplest of terms. The key to success in any long-distance phone company, he explains, is of course to build and grow a customer base. Market leaders such as AT&T, MCI, and Sprint do this by taking a chunk of the revenues generated from those customers—$3 million a day, to be exact—and then spending it on expensive television advertising campaigns in order to get more customers. This has been the basic business approach since telephone deregulation and the breakup of the Bell system in 1984.

Excel does it differently. The company takes a big chunk of money generated from customers and returns it to its Independent Representatives, who in turn seek more customers through network marketing. Because a new phone customer is buying something from a friend or family member rather than from a celebrity on a TV ad, Excel is building the most loyal customer base the communications industry has ever seen.

"It's a win, win, win situation," Steve assures the audience. The customers win because they're getting a good service at a lower price from someone they know and care about. The company wins because it's making a profit. And the Representatives win because they're building their own independent businesses with loyal customers and attractive long-term income potential.

Excel Today

The company Steve Schulz was describing that Friday night in Los Angeles has turned the telecommunications business on its ear.

Founded in 1988 by Kenny Troutt, chairman and chief executive officer, Excel has quickly become one of the fastest-growing providers of long-distance communications. The company currently serves four million long-distance telephone customers, who used 6.3 billion minutes of calling time in 1996; these numbers will expand significantly upon consummation of Excel's recently announced plan to acquire Telco Communications Group. With about 3 percent of the market, Excel is America's fifth-largest long-distance provider in terms of presubscribed lines.

It earned that status and customer base not by developing its own switching and transmission networks but by purchasing blocks of long-distance time and value-added services at deep discounts from the primary carriers and reselling it to end users.

Excel's growth has been astounding. In 1996, the company's revenues totaled $1.4 billion, a 167 percent increase over 1995. Only two other start-up companies on record have climbed their way past the $1 billion mark as fast as Excel. In May 1996, Excel became one of the youngest companies ever to be listed on the New York Stock Exchange.

Today, Excel is the company everyone is talking about both in communications and in network marketing. Indeed, it is the company's union of these two powerful industries that has resulted in its unique character and formula for success.

Setting the Stage: Growth and Change in Telecommunications

Excel would not exist today were it not for society's insatiable appetite for the telephone and an ever-expanding array of communications products and services. The telephone and the industries it has spawned have been revolutionizing our society for more than 120 years, and they show no sign of letting up.

It all began when 29-year-old Alexander Graham Bell walked into the patent office on February 14, 1876, to file an application for his new invention: the telephone.

Bell had always been fascinated by the patterns of speech and sound, and he had good reason to be. His grandfather was a professor of elocution. His father was a linguist who taught speech to the deaf and invented a phonetic alphabet called Visible Speech. Bell's mother was deaf, but she was also a talented pianist who was able to "hear" music she played by placing the mouthpiece of her ear tube on the sounding board. It was the realization that sound could travel along wires that created the first sparks of the idea for the telephone in the inventor's mind.

One day, while attempting to read a treatise on sound by a German scientist, written in German, Bell misunderstood the text to say that vowels could be reproduced electromagnetically and could travel over a wire. (What the treatise really reported was that vowels could be reproduced by a combination of electrical tuning forks and resonators.)

With this skewed notion in mind, the inventor found financial support from interested investors and started working on a harmonic telegraph, a system that would allow more than one message at a time to travel over a telegraph line. At the time, telegraphs were unable to send more than a single message in a single direction at one time, causing messages to back up for hours.

Bell needed help with the mechanical aspects of his idea, so he hired Thomas A. Watson as his assistant. The pair worked diligently for months, conducting experiment after experiment to develop the harmonic telegraph. The only problem was that it didn't work!

Bell then shifted his focus to an intriguing tangent: Why couldn't *any* sound travel over the telegraph? Bell reasoned that if he could make a current of electricity vary in intensity, precisely as the air varies in density during the production of a sound, he should be able to transmit speech telegraphically.

His investors weren't interested, however. They demanded results on the harmonic telegraph, so further work on what was to be become the telephone became a clandestine operation.

A key challenge was quickly isolated. Bell had to find a substance that would deliver the current necessary to transmit actual words. One day, he accidentally spilled battery acid on his telephone and on himself. He shouted, "Mr. Watson, come here! I want you!" Bell's voice carried over the phone. It was the phone call heard round the world!

Never a Down Quarter

Thus was born the industry that Excel leader Meg Kelly-Smith points out "has never had a down quarter in over a century."

The invention initially had its doubters and cynics, though. The chief of the British Post Office was reported to have said: "The Americans may have need for the telephone, but we do not. We have plenty of messenger boys."

Mark Twain dismissed the new contraption with this legendary put-down: "If Bell had invented a muffler or gag, he would have done a real service."

Others reacted with fear and superstition. They were afraid to talk to a disembodied voice and worried they would be electrocuted. Still others felt the phone was simply another "gilded-age" toy for the upper crust—certainly not a development that would alter the lives of average people and society as a whole.

"Telephones are rented only to persons of good breeding and refinement," an early advertisement reminded potential customers. Indeed, it cost a fortune: $150 to lease a telephone in New York and $100 in Chicago and Philadelphia. That was a lot of money in the 1880s. True to that "good breeding and refinement" mentality, many early customers hid their phones in a cupboard or installed a special cabinet to house the instrument.

Even the now universal method of answering the telephone went through several manifestations in the very early days. Alexander Graham Bell always said "Ahoy!" When Thomas Edison worked on perfecting the device, it had to be cranked first and the user asked "Are you there?" Edison thought that took too long, so he just said "Hello?"

The early notion that the telephone would remain an extravagance for a small segment of society was quickly proved wrong. Communications technology spread like wildfire from day one, and it hasn't stopped since:

- In 1878, the first telephone was installed in the White House during the Rutherford B. Hayes administration. The president's first call was to Bell, who was 13 miles away. Hayes had to ask him to talk more slowly.
- In 1880, the first public pay station in the world began service. For 10 cents paid to a uniformed attendant, one could call anyone who had a phone.
- In 1892, telephone lines linked New York and Chicago.
- By 1902, the U.S. had 2.1 million telephones. Just 12 years later, in 1914, that number had multiplied to 10 million.

o In 1911, New York and Denver were linked.
o On January 25, 1915, the first coast-to-coast telephone call took place, appropriately between Alexander Graham Bell in New York and Thomas A. Watson in San Francisco.
o In 1921, the first rotary dial came into use.
o In 1927, the first overseas call took place.
o In 1929, Herbert Hoover became the first U.S. president to have a phone on his desk in the Oval Office.

Today, 150 million telephone lines are in service in America, and the usage works out to every man, woman, and child in America spending 40 minutes a day on the phone. Analysts keep looking for the saturation point, but thanks to dramatic technological developments, new products, and insatiable customer demand, no one sees it anywhere on the horizon. Consider the industry of which Excel is a part:

o Operating revenues for all telephone communication services exceeded $195 billion annually— a 22 percent increase in just four years.
o Local, long-distance, network access, cellular service, and international calling have all been growing at double-digit or even triple-digit rates through the first half of the 1990s.
o Since 1990, long-distance calling, which still accounts for nearly 40 percent of revenues, has

grown 15 percent; local calling has grown by
17 percent.

o International calling has skyrocketed, with the
number of calls increasing more than 600 percent
since 1980. In 1994, Americans spent at least
$12.4 billion on 2.3 billion international calls.

o In 1994, 27 million people carried pagers. In just
three years that number has increased to 40 million. By the year 2000, it is expected to exceed
70 million.

o Ten years ago, just over two million Americans
had cellular phones. Today, nearly 34 million
do. While average monthly phone bills have
been dropping due to cheaper, more competitively priced service, total revenues in the
cellular phone market have increased tenfold in
just a decade.

o The number of 800 numbers in use has more
than doubled from 1993 to 1995 alone. Nearly
seven million are in use today, and we're running
out of numbers. In 1995, a new number (888)
was created, along with 15 additional standard
area codes in that year alone.

o Even ancillary endeavors, such as the publishing
of directories, have become hugely profitable
businesses. According to *Once Upon a Telephone*,
by Ellen Stern and Emily Gwathmey, the first
telephone directory had six business headings.
Today it has over 5,000. By 1994, there were

200 Yellow Pages publishers in the United States, organizing, collating, printing, and distributing over 350 million phone directories and generating over $9.3 billion in annual revenue.

From Monopoly to Market Mayhem

It may seem like an anomaly, but an industry based on continual advances in state-of-the-art technology has also been, for much of its existence, a government-regulated monopoly.

All that has changed. Today, it's one of the most competitive, innovative, and entrepreneurial businesses in the world, with thousands of upstart companies dropping in and dropping out. Consumers, for the most part, are in the catbird's seat: despite initial confusion and sometimes annoying sales pitches interrupting the family dinner, prices are generally going down, while the range, quality, and accessibility of services are going up. Here's how it happened.

In 1934, Congress established the Federal Communications Commission (FCC), an agency regulating AT&T's legal monopoly on the following:

- ○ The manufacturing of all phones, cables, and communications products through its Western Electric Company

○ All scientific research and product development through its Bell Telephone Laboratories

○ All long-distance service

State Public Utilities Commissions (PUCs) were charged with regulating local telephone service.

Both AT&T's monopoly and the regulatory oversight was viewed as the most efficient way of achieving universal access and service. In addition, high capital costs related to the installation of the telephone network, as well as the labor intensity of the business, created a conventional wisdom that maintained the following three points:

1. AT&T deserved some market protection to ensure it could eventually turn a profit on its huge infrastructure investments.

2. No other serious player could afford to enter the market competitively anyway.

3. Segments of the country and the populous would be left without service without government regulation.

Between the 1930s and the early 1970s, several fissures in the monopoly's foundation began to appear. In 1956, the government issued a Consent Decree prohibiting AT&T from developing new businesses and thus taking advantage of the protection it enjoyed.

In 1969, a company called Microwave Communications Inc.—better known as MCI—was allowed to offer private-line service between Chicago and St. Louis. Two years later, the FCC opened up the key private-line market to other common carriers in addition to MCI.

The year 1974 saw the beginning of a long ending to AT&T's monopoly, with an antitrust lawsuit by rival MCI. Eight months later, the Justice Department launched a more comprehensive legal assault on AT&T's entire monopoly structure. It was this case that nearly a decade later would lead to the breakup of the company, the spawning of literally thousands of upstart competitors, and the birth of Excel.

Yet, during this drawn-out process, AT&T's monopoly enjoyed strong support from both parties in Congress, most of big business, the FCC, state PUCs, the Department of Defense, individual companies, and organized labor. So why did support crumble? As detailed in Jeremy Turnstall's *Communications Deregulation,* while MCI fired the first shots, AT&T was in fact beaten by three factors:

Technology: It proved increasingly difficult to control the technology, as scientific advances were made almost daily. Big businesses increasingly began to see the company as technologically backward rather than innovative, and they complained that AT&T failed to recognize their needs for sophistication in communications.

Consumers, accustomed to a plethora of choices in other product and service industries, had grown tired of the availability of one or two models of telephones and so few options on the service menu.

Inflation: Persistent inflation through much of the 1970s meant that AT&T was continually having to ask for, and increasingly having to fight for, rate increases. Monopolistic protection accompanied by government-set and -sanctioned rates discourages efficiency and encourages bloat and bureaucracy.

Politics: During the 1970s and early 1980s, AT&T's leadership was defeated politically by failing to anticipate that repeated exposure to the glare of congressional committee hearings would steadily sap its strength in lobbying and public image. As it fought its court battles, the company pulled out all the stops in Congress to prevent legislation-mandated deregulation.

While such legislation was prevented, AT&T found itself swimming against a strong current. Sweeping deregulation plans affecting aviation, trucking, and other industries were picking up steam and would be enacted by the end of the 1970s.

In 1981, both AT&T and the Justice Department asked Judge Harold Greene for a postponement of the long-awaited *U.S. v. AT&T* antitrust trial. Judge Greene denied the request. The company saw the writing on the wall. Faced with the prospect of endless indecisive legislative battles, plus the prospect of a hostile verdict from Judge Greene and other lawsuits to follow, AT&T agreed to a Justice-approved divestiture plan on January 8, 1982. In 1984, the breakup of AT&T's regulated monopoly was completed. The company divested itself of the 22 local Bell system operating companies, which accounted for the bulk of its revenues, profits, and one million employees.

It was the end of an era—and the beginning of a wild ride into the future.

Enter the Upstarts

"Bungled forays into computers, online services, and multimedia ventures are an old story at AT&T, but its core long-distance business was supposed to be a market the company had down cold. Not anymore," *Business Week* recently concluded. In fact, the post-monopoly world has been a tough place for the telephone giant.

Since 1984, AT&T's traffic has grown at a rate slower than the industry average. The result has been a declining share of the interstate market, as measured in minutes—from over 80 percent then to about 56 percent by 1995. The company's share of long-distance revenues suffered an equally precipitous decline—from over 90 percent in 1984 to 55 percent a decade later.

Even so, the initial phase of the deregulated long-distance phone market was marked by the emergence of several big players—what *Business Week* calls the "oligopoly" of AT&T, MCI, and Sprint. As recently as 1995, they controlled 90 percent of the market.

It was competitive, to be sure. Who could forget the multimillion-dollar television ad wars the giants of the industry launched against one another to sway the loyalties of customers? To most of us, the competitive noise was confusing and annoying. We simply tuned it out.

Today, thanks to companies like Excel, the oligopoly has fallen apart just as the monopoly did some 15 years ago. "Tiny rivals are grabbing customers and blindsiding the telecom giant [AT&T]," notes *Business Week*. "And poised on the horizon are the massive Baby Bells, waiting for regulators to allow them into long distance." In fact, by the spring of 1997, with both local and long-distance service opened to an entirely new set of players, another expensive television ad war has broken out all over the country. This time, the protagonists are local phone companies protecting their market shares by condemning long-distance providers, and long-distance giants like AT&T defending their turf.

States *Los Angeles Times* business columnist James Flanigan: "Since 1984, when AT&T's regulated monopoly was broken up, smaller companies have been responsible for virtually all advances in telecommunications."

This has shaken investor confidence in AT&T. The company's public image had already taken a beating when it announced a massive layoff in 1996. (Some of the downsized AT&T employees have since joined Excel as Independent Representatives.) Today, investors see AT&T's phone business coming under siege faster than anyone had expected. Prepaid calling cards and Internet calling, once it is perfected, pose additional risks for AT&T or for any company that lacks the reflexes to respond to a constantly changing business.

There's no question that AT&T is looking over its shoulder at companies like Excel. Imitation is indeed the sincerest form of flattery. That's the reaction at Excel to AT&T's recently announced partnership with Shaklee for the purpose of building a network marketing component into its business.

Excel's Business Strategy

The long-distance portion of telecommunications is already an $80-billion-a-year industry growing at a rate of $500 million a month. In a climate of rapid growth, deregulation, and intense competition, Excel has flourished, thanks to a unique business strategy.

First, the company has targeted two significant segments of the market:

1. Residential customers—those who individually spend less than $500 a month on long distance

but who together make up more than 50 percent of the long-distance market

2. Commercial service for small and medium-sized businesses

Second, rather than incurring the tremendous capital expense of installing its own telephone network, Excel essentially kick-started its entry into the business by purchasing long-distance calling capacity from network-based companies at deep discounts and reselling it to customers.

Third, instead of hiring an expensive in-house, employee-based sales force and buttressing it with a costly national advertising campaign, Excel markets and distributes products exclusively through a network of tens of thousands of Independent Representatives (often called IRs).

Relationship selling is the basis of the business opportunity Excel offers to these Representatives. Excel Representatives are encouraged to build their own home-based business by seeking subscribers among their immediate circles of family, friends, business associates, and acquaintances. It is therefore ironic that some industry analysts have called companies like Excel "Brand X" companies because their name is not as familiar to the public at large as the big three (AT&T, MCI, and Sprint). In the Excel plan, you as a customer are liable to have as your long-distance provider your own father, mother, son, or daughter. Who would call a family member or loved one "Brand X"? In this fashion, Excel has put loyalty back into the long-distance telephone business.

Fourth, Excel's products stress simplicity and continuity, which are important attractions for today's confused telephone consumers.

Unlike other calling plans, nothing changes when a phone customer switches to Excel, except the savings he or she realizes. The customer picks up the phone and dials one plus the area code and number, just as before. The call gets routed through the local exchange carrier and on to a national digital fiber network.

Most customers will notice no change in their billing either, since Excel has established billing contracts with most of the local providers who issue the bills. Adding to customer convenience is the fact that there is no minimum usage requirement. Savings begin with the very first phone call.

In addition to what Excel terms "Simply One" calling, the company offers a range of other communications services and products that are constantly being expanded and upgraded. They include the following:

o Discounted long-distance residential calling
o Discounted long-distance commercial calling
o 800 service
o International calling
o Calling cards
o Paging products and services

In the works are plans to enter the local telephone market and key international markets and to offer banking services and residential electricity.

The Excel Opportunity

While the company offers discounted, quality telecommunications services to its customers, it offers Representatives a low-cost, home-based business opportunity based on the principles of network marketing.

By gathering a few customers and convincing a few others to do the same, the Excel Independent Representative begins earning immediate cash income by receiving a percentage of those customers' long-distance usage each and every month. There are also cash bonuses for bringing customers and other Representatives' customers into the business quickly, stipends for training others on the company's behalf, and an escalating schedule of financial incentives, which grows as the Representative increases the network of people he or she brings into the business.

Immediate cash income, serious income potential and long-term residual income, and the great satisfaction that comes from building one's own business—these are the rewards that are today attracting tens of thousands of people to Excel. You can enjoy these rewards and the following benefits as well:

○ There are no deliveries and no inventory.

○ You collect no money from customers—local companies or Excel does that for you.

○ There is no customer risk. If for any reason a customer is dissatisfied with the service, Excel will reimburse any charge for switching back.

○ You have no employees, which means you don't have to worry about withholding, workers compensation, or workers calling in sick.

○ You are not an employee either. You don't work for anyone but yourself.

○ You can build your business by gathering customers and new Representatives anywhere, not just where you live.

○ No experience is necessary. Excel will provide you with all the training you need.

When some consider opening their own businesses, one of the first opportunities they look at is a franchise. According to *Entrepreneur* magazine, typical start-up fees for franchises can range anywhere from a low end of $3,000 for a shopping-bag advertising company to a midrange of $60,000 for an antique and custom furniture franchise to a high end of $200,000 and up for a fancy car-wash business.

How much does it cost to start an Excel business? There is a fully refundable $50 application deposit to become an Independent Representative, for which you receive the basic materials and information.

However, those serious about getting off on the right foot choose to become Managing Representatives. This status provides an IR with training, a home office support system, newsletters, and Excel's bookkeeping and accounting services. There is a one-time $195 charge to become a Managing Representative, in which case the $50 deposit is waived, with an annual renewal of $180.

So, for less than $200 at the outset and less than $200 per year, you can be in business for yourself. All you need to know is a few people with a phone who might want to do you a favor by switching to a lower-cost long-distance provider that saves them money! It's not rocket science—just the genius of common sense.

Matching Growth with Stature

By turning the "people power" of network marketing loose on the booming, deregulated telecommunications industry, and by reselling high-quality service at a lower price rather than launching its own capital-intensive telephone system, Excel has made a fast and significant mark in the business world.

Yet when you're living on the freewheeling frontier, as Excel has done for the past nine years, there comes a time when it's important to put down roots. In addition to its initial public offering on the New York Stock Exchange, in the last several years the company has taken other important steps to position itself for long-term growth.

Excel is a solid professional corporation with a top management team and 2,200 employees in its Dallas headquarters and its call centers in both Houston and Addison, Texas, as well as in Reno, Nevada.

It has added seasoned executive talent to its management team, such as Jack McLaine, now the company's president and chief operating officer. Jack was hired as the company's chief financial officer in August 1994, after a distinguished career that included running his own firm, which provided merger and acquisition services to *Fortune* 500 companies. He has served as chief financial officer and president of international operations for Pearle Vision Inc. and as a vice president for American National Can Co.

His ascension to the position of Excel president and COO comes on the heels of his successful management of two major company milestones: its initial public offering in 1996 and its merger agreement with Telco Communications Group in June 1997. The role Jack plays as a strategic counselor and trusted business confidant for chairman and CEO Kenny Troutt became clear from my very first visit to Excel. During my initial meeting with Kenny, Jack was by his side, offering his cogent analysis and thoughtful insights into the reasons for Excel's success and the challenges that lie ahead.

Says Kenny Troutt of Jack McLaine: "Jack has a unique ability to view the Excel business model from a global perspective, and to evaluate product markets and services while bringing all the business elements together. Under his leadership, we'll continue to set the standard in the communications industry."

The company's plan to build its own switching and transmission network through the purchase of state-of-the-art switches from Lucent Technologies, as well as its decision to acquire Telco, begins a new era for the young company—an evolutionary development from a reseller to a facilities-based carrier that will allow Excel to become a major competitor in a much larger universe of communications services and products.

Communications and network marketing. It's a winning combination. Yet it didn't happen by accident. Like Alexander Graham Bell and Thomas A. Watson more than 120 years ago, the match was made because of the vision and drive of a determined leader, Kenny Troutt, and a dedicated partner, Steve Smith.

— Excel at its heart is a people business. Its most valuable product is not telephone service but service to others, giving each person in the business the chance to achieve his or her dreams by helping others achieve theirs. It is impossible to fully understand the business, why it works, and where it's going without probing the ideas, motivations, backgrounds, and dreams of the key people who saw the vision and acted upon it.

I'd like to introduce some of them to you in the chapters to come.

RINGING THE BELL

FRIDAY, MAY 10, 1996, 9:30 A.M. on the nose. The clang, clang of the bell signaling the opening of the day's trading on the New York Stock Exchange rings out over the floor. Ringing the bell is Kenny Troutt, afforded the ceremonial honor because Excel Communications, the company he founded and leads, begins its first day of public trading, with an offering of 11.5 million shares of common stock.

"As I watched our symbol, ECI, flow across the display board of the world's most prestigious securities exchange," Kenny said later, "I was reminded of what this giant step means to Excel. This was a momentous day in our company's history."

And it was a momentous day in the life of Kenny Troutt. Stock offered at $15 per share nearly doubled in price on that first day of trading, effectively jettisoning the 48-year-old Texas entrepreneur into the ranks of America's billionaires with the clang, clang of the closing bell.

A Long Way from Home

It was a long way from the public housing project in Mount Vernon, Illinois, where Kenny's mother—affectionately known as Mama Nadine throughout the Excel family—worked as a school cook and struggled to raise her three kids in the 1950s. "It was a rougher neighborhood than any of us can imagine," Kenny's wife, Lisa, tells us today. Crime, violence, drugs, and hoodlum activity were part of the daily life.

Almost from the start, Mama Nadine saw something different in her oldest son. By age two, the strong will and intense curiosity were already shining through. As the young boy grew and became aware of his poor surroundings, he developed a strong drive to escape those surroundings through entrepreneurship.

"Other boys were idolizing sports heroes and dreaming of the day they could lift themselves up that way," Kenny recalls. "But I remember reading about America's richest people in *Forbes* and *Fortune* and wanting to be just like them. They were my heroes." One day, when Kenny was in the fourth grade, his teacher asked the students in class what they wanted to be when they grew up. Some said a fire fighter; others said a doctor. Kenny Troutt replied, "I want to be rich."

By age seven, Kenny started his first business. He organized neighborhood bike races, enticed contestants with a winner's trophy, which he made himself, and charged them 25 cents for the privilege of competing. He made a handsome profit.

At 11 years of age, Kenny went into the movie theater business—by building a clubhouse in his backyard, locating an old projector and some home movies, and charging kids 25 cents for a show, popcorn, and a Coke.

Two years later, the young entrepreneur established a lawn mowing business. He bought mowers, hired his brothers and cousins as employees, and went out and enlisted customers. This was another profit-making venture.

Kenny says he learned from these early experiences the enormous difference just one or two hundred dollars can make in most people's lives. Faced with the obstacles of a rough neighborhood, an absent father, and the responsibility as the oldest son to help support his family, a youthful Kenny Troutt had two paths to choose from. He could allow himself to sink into the despair of his surroundings, helplessly eyeing from afar with bitterness and envy those who were better off. Or, through hard work and ingenuity, he could clear a path of escape out of the housing projects to a life full of opportunities.

Why do so many of us passively accept the circumstances we are born into, while others like Kenny Troutt simply refuse to let anything defeat or deter their escape and rise to the top? Kenny credits his mother, a special aunt, and his school coaches for guiding him to the right path.

For a poor boy from the projects, the only path to college was through a scholarship. And the only path to a scholarship for a student with less-than-stellar grades was through sports. "In my neighborhood, sports was really the only vehicle to get out and make it to college," Kenny told me. A football scholarship was his vehicle to Southern Illinois University.

He excelled in sports in college as he had done in high school, but with money tight and the entrepreneurial drive still churning inside, it wasn't very long before Kenny Troutt was back in business again. College roommate Pete Wittmann—and 30 years later, still one of Kenny's closest friends—recalls that "he did anything he could to make a buck. He had to." To help pay for room and board, Kenny worked as the breakfast cook in their fraternity. "He worked unloading trucks. He sold watermelons. No job was too good, no job was too bad," Pete recalls. There were even a few outings to the track. "Because we both loved horses," Pete says slyly.

"The thing you have to understand about Kenny is that being deprived as a child gave him this tremendous drive to be successful," Pete continues. "He had surrounded himself with successful people long before he was a success. He wanted to be just like them."

Think back on your college days. You're in your senior year, and it's countdown time to graduation. Maybe you're cramming to turn in a thesis. Perhaps there will be time for a backpack trip to Europe in the summer. What kind of job can you land in the fall with your new degree? How will you pay off the student loans?

Kenny Troutt didn't wait for graduation to begin the transition from student to working professional. While a senior in college, he got a job selling insurance and quickly became his company's top salesman, earning $75,000 a year. That was a lot of money around 1970—and it's nothing to sneeze at today!

As good as he was, when Kenny inquired about an executive job with the company, he was told that "he wasn't good managerial material." The young man was furious, Pete Wittmann recalls. Especially when shortly afterwards a business magazine ranked the nation's insurance companies in terms of quality and performance, and his company was at the very bottom of the list! So much for its ability to recognize "good managerial material."

The experience underscored one lesson Kenny would remember later when forming Excel: "One of my goals is to run a *Fortune* 500 company. Nobody's going to hire me to run one. So I've got to build one."

Graduating from the university in 1970, Kenny threw himself into a wide array of entrepreneurial activities, from real estate development to a basement waterproofing business. He moved to Omaha, Nebraska, and started his own construction company, making big money for the first time. "But he plowed a lot of those profits into a thoroughbred horse farm," his friend and frequent business partner Pete explains. "And his ingenuity showed through there, too. You see, the winters were so long and cold in Nebraska that most of the racehorses were unable to train and build up their strength until spring, and start of the racing season was almost upon us. What Kenny did was construct a pool for the horses to swim in during the winter, so they were in far better shape far sooner than others.

"Kenny's horses would be entered in races at 50-to-1 odds and win!"

The Road to Texas

Not everything went smoothly, however. The overhead costs in the thoroughbred business were tremendous, and in the late 1970s interest rates soared into the stratosphere—a less-than-ideal climate for construction and real estate development, to say the least. There were some tough financial losses. On the personal side, a first attempt at marital bliss ended in divorce.

So by the end of the 1970s, Kenny was ready for a new frontier. He chose Dallas and the oil industry. With his dog, Ginger, as a companion, he loaded up his belongings in his truck and made his way south to

Texas. When the truck broke down on the way, Kenny baled hay to make enough money to continue his journey.

Knowing virtually nothing about oil, Kenny began working for a company selling oil wells. Following a now familiar pattern, he was tremendously successful, attracting investors such as Pete Wittmann, Bill and Susan Casner, and Fred and Charlotte Parrill. Like Mama Nadine years before, they noticed something different and rare in Kenny Troutt. Fred Parrill remembers: "He was a person of total integrity—a real professional. Anyone who has ever had anything to do with him is awestruck by his sincerity and how hard he works." Echoes Fred's wife, Charlotte, "If Kenny Troutt says he's going to do something, he'll do it. It's as simple as that. In our view, it wasn't that we were investing in oil or later in Excel. What we were really investing in was Kenny."

In fact, their faith proved so unshakable that even when the oil boom turned to bust and they took a financial beating, they were first in line to invest in Kenny Troutt's next big idea: telecommunications.

Kenny eyed the breakup of AT&T closely, believing from the start that deregulation, combined with emerging new affordable personal communications technologies, would trigger a boom "that would make the oil boom look like a poverty zone." Experiencing years of tremendous highs and tremendous lows in businesses like insurance, construction, and oil had taught the indefatigable entrepreneur some vital lessons.

"There came a point where I had to sit down and think about what I wanted to do for the rest of my life. I wanted a business where you get paid down the road with residual income. I was looking for a product that everyone needed, had, or used. And I wanted to be in an industry where as hard as I looked I couldn't see any limitations.

"It was 1988, and that's when I started Excel." Asked if he could recall a precise moment of inspiration when the idea burst into his brain, Kenny humbly waves off the suggestion. He credits his brother with giving him the idea of breaking into the industry by being a switchless reseller. He credits Steve Smith for introducing the network marketing approach to the business. And he is clearly grateful to Jack McLaine for steering the company through its initial public offering on Wall Street and the Telco merger. Drawing the best ideas from the best people around him—and giving them credit for their contributions—was and is an appealing Troutt trademark.

But at the beginning what Kenny Troutt needed the most was money.

"I remember after the price of oil went from about $50 a barrel down to $15, Kenny called me up all excited," Pete Wittmann told me. "He said, 'Send me all the money you've got. You and I are going to get mega-rich! How much have you got, anyway?'"

Pete told Kenny he had about $20,000 in the bank and maybe another $20,000 in available credit on his bank cards. "Send it all," Kenny told him.

"So I did, all forty grand worth—without telling my wife," Pete says. "Soon as I did that I started working extra and on weekends to pay back those credit cards before she found out."

Bill Casner was ready to help as well. He had met Kenny in Omaha 25 years earlier (he and wife, Susan, have been close friends of the Troutt family ever since). "After we both gravitated to Texas, we got into the oil business together," Bill told me. "And we were doing very well until the bottom fell out of oil prices.

"One night, Kenny called me all excited about the telecommunications business. He was convinced this was finally going to be the home run he had been looking for."

Bill remembers Excel in the very early days. "The whole company consisted of a 150-square-foot office, a couple of desks, and a couple of phones," he says. "I remember when Kenny was the only employee. He answered the phones, he negotiated the contracts to buy long-distance minutes, and he went out and signed up the customers. He did everything."

An original Excel investor, Bill felt the odds of success were long. "I knew Kenny was like no other person I had met and that he would give it his life blood to make it work. I could live with losing my money, but I could not endure watching it hit without me. It had the potential like nothing I had ever been involved in. We were really undercapitalized. We had less than $400,000 when we should have had $3 million. I think the money problem Excel faced at the outset is one reason Kenny became so determined later to offer Independent Representatives a chance to get into business without a lot of capital. It's such a handicap for most small businesses—but not for Excel businesses."

The Parrills, the Casners, and Dan and Linda Martignon all stepped up to the plate, too. "Kenny was so excited," Charlotte Parrill recalls. "But he didn't pull any punches. He warned us there were no guarantees. But we had so much faith in Kenny that we took all our money out of our savings and just handed it over."

"There were no contracts, no signatures. We knew we didn't need to be concerned about that," adds Fred.

Today, living comfortably on the wealth they've realized from that simple act of trust and loyalty ten years ago, the Parrills call themselves "the classic Cinderella story."

For Dan and Linda Martignon, Excel represents the one investment that finally worked out. After his first wife passed away in 1982, "I started making some wild-type investments," Dan remembers. "In fact, I've got a three-ring binder listing all the projects that failed." One such project was an oil well that the company he invested in couldn't afford to cap. "Kenny Troutt came in and agreed to take it over and cap it in exchange for the mailing list of investors. I met Kenny when he contacted me from that list," Dan told me.

"Kenny really took me under his wing. We invested in an oil well together, and I remember driving out with him in the morning to see if it was going to be a success. As we approached, Kenny saw the rig being dismantled and knew right then it had failed."

It was on the trip back that Kenny started talking about his new idea in telecommunications. To Dan, who had spent much of his professional career working as an area manager for Southwestern Bell, his ideas sounded crazy. "I told Kenny he was nuts," Dan says. "Kenny told me he understood and that when we sold our oil lease I could either get my money back or invest in his idea. I thought about it for a second and said, 'Okay, I'm in.'"

Why was Dan willing to take such a chance—even after losing money on the gusher that never gushed? "When Kenny decides to do something, he always goes after it one thousand percent. He always follows through and cares about each and every investor. I just couldn't take the chance not to be involved."

Today, at age 58, Dan is taking an early retirement to help raise four grandchildren. He and his wife, Linda, have found Excel gatherings a rich source of lasting friendships. It's such a valuable part of our lives, and I'm not talking about the money," Dan says. Linda and I are really caught up in the excitement of how this business is turning people's lives around."

As for Pete Wittmann, he is still trying to forget the day back in 1993 when he told his wife that they now had enough saved to cash in their original shares in Excel. "She wanted to. I didn't," Pete told me. "But to be accommodating, I agreed to sell enough to at least get back the original $40,000 we put in." Later, after the company went public and a market value was established for his remaining piece of the company, Pete realized it was a decision that cost him millions of dollars!

As for Kenny, the former frat-house breakfast cook— is Pete surprised that his friend is now a billionaire? "Not at all," Pete says. "It doesn't surprise me one bit.

"But he's still the same guy he always was, and so am I. Recently, I had a bad day at the track and lost $700. That same day I found out that the stock market took a tumble and the value of my Excel stock dropped, on paper anyway, by millions of dollars. I told Kenny, 'You know something, that $700 I lost at the track hurts more!'"

Finding Real Happiness

As Kenny was building Excel, propelling it to unprecedented growth and helping thousands find personal happiness through entrepreneurship, a chance meeting through friends changed his life in a wonderful way. He met Lisa.

"I grew up in a small town near Houston," Lisa recalls. "We were three children from a close and loving family. We were fortunate that our mother could stay home with us. My father owned his own business and worked long hours, yet he was constantly encouraging and motivating us to follow our dreams."

Lisa attended the University of North Texas in Denton and graduated with a degree in fashion design. She then began a successful and enjoyable career in Dallas working for major apparel companies. "I loved the business, but I always knew my focus would eventually be on raising a family.

"When I met Kenny I knew right away that there was something very different and special about him." To this day she marvels at the fact that when they met, all he told her was that he worked for a long-distance telephone company. "That's what he told everyone. When he met them, he never bragged that he started the company or that he was the CEO."

After dating for a short time, Kenny and Lisa knew they had each found the real thing. The couple was married in 1993. Today, they are the proud parents of two young sons, Preston Allen Troutt and Grant Michael Troutt. The family recently moved into a beautiful new home in one of Dallas's most prestigious neighborhoods.

Even though building Excel into the *Fortune* 500 company Kenny dreams it to be consumes enormous amounts of his time and energies, Lisa looks at the positive side. "Excel has brought so many people into our lives. This company is all about touching people's lives. It's taking the time to listen and caring enough to help."

Despite family responsibilities and numerous functions and appearances related to the business, Lisa has not lost her focus on how the company can impact the life of a single individual. During the company's annual "Excelebration" convention in September 1996, she emotionally told the story of misfortune that had befallen a friend.

"Just before we moved into our new house, a good friend of mine who ran a showroom at the Apparel Mart called, and she was very distraught. Her father-in-law was in the hospital and not expected to live. She had to go and be with her family, but she was worried about her business. Could I help?"

With two young children at home, it was the worst possible time for Lisa—"But a good friend would be there."

At the showroom, one of the employees Lisa supervised had not been working for very long and was seven months pregnant. Her husband had been unemployed for a year. "They had no health insurance and were going to garage sales to find maternity clothes. She wasn't complaining. She was telling me this cheerfully," Lisa says.

The first thing Lisa did was bring in some of her old maternity clothes for the young woman. "Then I told her all about Excel, how she could work at home with her new baby and really change her family's life." Since this woman's husband had been a teacher and a coach, Lisa reflected on the fact that Excel's top money earner, Paul Orberson, was a former high school coach who had never made more than $35,000 a year at his previous job. Lisa told the young employee, "You know something? Teachers and coaches have a really good track record in Excel!"

Paraphrasing a passage from Proverbs, Lisa Troutt believes "It is possible to give away and become richer. It is also possible to hold on too tightly and lose everything." There is no better exercise for the heart than reaching down and lifting people up."

In speaking to Kenny Troutt, giving people a chance is clearly the mission that defines Excel. "What our approach brings to the table," he told me, "is a chance for everyone to change their lives. Eighty-five percent of new businesses go broke in less than five years. So what we've tried to do for our Independent Representatives is to clear as many obstacles from their path as possible. You don't need an inventory. You don't have to understand distribution, warehousing, or shipping, and you don't have to be an expert in telecommunications. All you have to do is see the vision.

"Unlike a product such as cosmetics, which you could argue is only used by a maximum of 50 percent of the people, everyone has a telephone. Everyone knows how to use the telephone, and they're already spending money on it." Kenny emphasizes the simplicity of the business. "When our Reps go out to get customers, they're not even asking those customers for any money. Just use our service."

If one expects to hear corporate buzzword babble or abstract, intellectual posturing from this chief executive, they can look elsewhere. Kenny Troutt is plainspoken and direct, and he exudes confidence and conviction with everything he says.

"It took me a couple of years to figure out how I could play their game," he says of Excel's giant competitors. "Now, to varying degrees, they're all trying to copy our approach and take our business.

"The problem they're going to have is that network marketing takes a special breed of people who are driven by different goals and dreams than people in the corporate world. The big companies won't allow that. In fact, in most major companies, once a salesperson makes too much, they either cut his territory or promote him to management."

Excel places no such limits on what an individual can achieve. With great satisfaction, Kenny notes that former high school coach Paul Orberson, Excel's top money earner, "makes more than the heads of AT&T, MCI, and Sprint put together!"

Yet Kenny is quick to emphasize that for most, money alone is not the driving force. "Most people can't relate to making a million dollars a year, and most people won't," he says. "But almost everybody can relate to achieving economic independence." He credits pioneering companies like Amway "for cleaning up the multilevel marketing business and paving the way for people like us." At the same time, he proudly notes Excel's relatively low attrition rate among its practitioners compared to other network marketing companies, as well as its unusually high appeal to upscale, white-collar professionals.

"When I started Excel, I had just read that 65 percent of all personal bankruptcies could be avoided if debtors had just an extra $185 a month in cash income," Kenny has said. "So I figured if I could find something that people could do to make just $150 or $200 extra per month, I could help change their lives."

In addition to bringing network marketing to telecommunications, Kenny believes another of Excel's big contributions is that "we're the first to get in front of and even ahead of the consumer on a one-to-one basis." By emphasizing sales to family members, friends, and associates, Excel Reps build up tremendous customer loyalty and a ready entree for the introduction of new products. Echoes Jack McLaine: "Relationship selling is the best way to sell long distance because of all the noise out there."

Perhaps most significant of all is that a company like Excel offers living proof that capitalism can thrive in a culture of "people helping people" rather than "dog eat dog." Steve Smith points out, "Since the very beginning and right up to the present day, there is no greater thrill for Kenny Troutt than to review each new list of payouts we've made to Reps. In many cases, we know how down they were in life when they started, and there's just no greater thrill for Kenny than to see them succeed."

"He truly believes his road to success is paved by helping others get there too," says Lisa Troutt about her husband.

New signposts of that success are popping up almost every day. From profiles in the publications *Success, Inc., Forbes,* and *Fortune* to being named the 1996 Southwest Area Entrepreneur of the Year and the Ernst and Young Entrepreneur of the Year, Kenny Troutt is quickly becoming a legend of American business.

Perhaps the most gratifying recognition of all occurred on October 14, 1996. That was the day *Forbes* issued its most recent list of the 400 richest people in America. On that list was a man who as a boy growing up poor pawed through the same magazine, vowing to himself, "Someday I'm going to be just like them!"

Where else but in America could a boy lying in bed in a housing project on the wrong side of the river dream of making it to the ranks of the nation's wealthiest people—and through hard work and an inexhaustible supply of entrepreneurial drive make that dream come true?

As young people today growing up in similar tough circumstances grasp for that one-in-a-billion chance of becoming the next sports hero or entertainment legend, we can only hope that more of them look up to Americans like Kenny Troutt. His dreams were built on the solid bedrock of American free enterprise, not on the near-impossible odds of professional sports or the fleecy clouds of Hollywood's dream factory. Dozens of people I talked to in the Excel business, from the spectacularly successful to those simply bringing in some helpful extra cash, are unabashed in their description of Kenny Troutt as "our hero." It's not a title Kenny carries comfortably. To this day, he admits being nervous whenever he gets up to make a speech, even when he's speaking to his most fervent fans.

For years our popular culture has vilified businesspeople. The higher they have climbed, the more viciously they have been portrayed. In a society that hungers for heroes and whose children desperately need positive role models, we should consider that some of the best candidates exist among our entrepreneurs, small business owners, and industry leaders, for what they represent are duplicable dreams, not virtually impossible fantasies.

What Makes a Leader?

What are the qualities that enable a leader like Kenny Troutt to build and steer a large company and inspire thousands to place their faith and hopes in his hands?

Generalities are hard to draw, and definitions of what constitutes a great leader change with the times. Sometimes we just know it when we see it. During my career, I have had many opportunities to personally observe many world leaders in a variety of settings.

In 1988, I sat four feet away from British Prime Minister Margaret Thatcher in 10 Downing Street as she passionately described the West's final struggle to free Eastern Europe and Russia from communism. I left the room absolutely awestruck, never having felt so confident that freedom would ultimately win out in that struggle.

In 1989, I watched Philippines President Corazon Aquino, who had already survived several coups and assassination attempts and whose husband had been gunned down several years earlier, sit serenely on a platform in a crowded Manila park waiting to give a speech. I was astounded by the apparent lack of security and the multitude of places an assassin could be hiding. As her generals and aides sat around her fanning themselves and sweating heavily in the 100-degree heat, Mrs. Aquino sat with a half-smile and not a bead of sweat on her face. She appeared to be in a state of complete tranquillity. Her quiet strength and courage amazed me.

I have been in receptions at the White House during both the Jimmy Carter and Ronald Reagan administrations, and I was struck by the different impact each president had. As President Carter entered the room, people were milling about and carrying on various conversations. Despite the president's presence, people kept right on talking. It was a full minute before they realized he was even there. Yet when President Reagan entered a similar venue several years later, no one missed his presence. The impact was immediate and the reverence palpable.

There may have been a time when Americans looked for flamboyance and even a degree of noblesse oblige from our leaders. Today, we still value those leaders who are strong, principled, courageous, and capable of conveying a vision that excites us and uplifts us. Yet we have little patience for arrogance and artificiality and for leaders who through their words, actions, and demeanor let us know how much better and smarter they are.

We want leaders who communicate to us, not down to us, leaders who understand the experiences and lives of average people but who still act like leaders.

During the many opportunities I have had to observe Kenny Troutt in recent months—in private meetings, before large groups, in his office, and in his home—I have tried to link the qualities that people see in him with those qualities I have observed in other leaders.

When he walks into a room, his presence is felt immediately: it's strong, direct, focused. He is sharply attired but is in no way flamboyant in either appearance, demeanor, or expression. When you're talking to Kenny Troutt, his focus is on you and his gaze is direct and probing. He is a good listener, but he does not patronize you by gratuitously agreeing with everything you say.

Many people in the Excel business used the words "focused" and "committed" to describe him. In my conversations with Kenny, I sense a person who knows exactly where he's going and what his goals are. He is a person who does not suffer fools gladly, whose simple, direct speech, unadorned by big words, could conceivably lull business competitors and others into thinking he's not as sharp or as crafty as they are—when in fact he's more likely to be three steps ahead of them!

The self-confidence, the ceaseless supply of energy, the plainspoken ability to motivate others, the sense you

get that he has never forgotten where he came from—
these are the qualities many have seen in Kenny Troutt.

Close friend Bill Casner has reflected carefully on the
traits that account for the Kenny Troutt brand of leadership and success. "First, it's the negotiating skills," Bill
says. "Kenny has nerves of steel. He's always willing to
walk away from the table if he has to. Second, Kenny has
endurance. No one can outwork him. No one can out-
last him, whether it's a marathon negotiating session or a
crash project needed to solve a problem or take advantage of an opportunity. Third, he has outstanding marketing skills. Fourth, he knows the numbers better than
anyone. He's a great number cruncher. Fifth, he thrives
on solving problems—and believe me, in the early years
of this business there are plenty for him to thrive on!

"Finally," Bill explains, "Kenny always makes sure
he takes a lot of people with him as he climbs the ladder of success. Whether they're investors or Representatives, he brings as many people along as he possibly
can. This has created thousands and thousands of
people who feel a tremendous loyalty to Kenny
Troutt—and he has earned it."

Success and wealth haven't changed him, Bill insists.
"I've known him for 25 years and he's the same Kenny
today that he was the first day I met him."

Indeed, you don't get the feeling you're talking to a
billionaire when you're talking to Kenny Troutt—but
you do know for sure that you are talking to a leader.

Calculating the Incalculable

Visitors to Excel's executive offices in Dallas today are struck by a large glass-enclosed display in the lobby containing photos, awards, and mementos marking the major milestones in the life and history of Kenny Troutt and Excel. Prominently and proudly featured as a centerpiece is a small desk calculator whose display goes only as high as nine digits. Kenny and his company rendered it obsolete the day they crossed the $1 billion milestone. It's there no doubt as a reminder of how far the Excel family has come. "Kenny will never forget where he came from," says his friend Fred Parrill.

Meanwhile, let's go back to that gathering of 1,500 current and prospective Excel Representatives in Los Angeles described at the beginning of chapter 1. Backstage, Kenny Troutt is concentrating on the speech he is about to make. His job is to share with the members of the audience his vision of the future of telecommunications and Excel and their place in that future. It's no small task. Meanwhile, Executive Directors Greg and Carolyn Beck approach him with a request. It seems that one of the Representatives in their group, an 82-year-old woman named Vivian Hankins from Tulare, California, who had been looking forward to the trip to Los Angeles, has instead been rushed to the hospital back home with a serious heart ailment.

"She lives for Excel," the Becks tell me. "She didn't start until she turned 81. Because she's in poor health, she does all her recruiting from home over the phone. She became a Senior Representative in just four months."

The Becks ask Kenny if he could call Vivian in the hospital, and he makes the call. "Vivian, this is Kenny Troutt. How are you feeling?" He looks up from the phone and says, "She's crying!"

Returning to the phone, Kenny tells Vivian, "Well, you get better so that next time you can come down here and yell and cheer even louder." He listens for a moment, then says, "I love you, too." He hangs up and embraces a staff member. Was he thinking about Mama Nadine, now in poor health and living in Florida? He returns to the auditorium and takes the stage.

"My mother always told me: 'On the way to the stars, take as many people with you as you can,'" says Kenny Troutt.

"THE MOST IMPRESSIVE THING I'VE EVER SEEN"

W HAT ACCOUNTS FOR Excel's meteoric rise in both business and telecommunications?

Clearly, Excel offers state-of-the-art telecommunications products and services for which the nation and the world have an insatiable demand—products that everyone uses, needs, and can understand.

Equally important is Excel's embrace of the fastest-growing approach to business in the world today: network marketing. The company has built upon the triumphs of the pioneers of network marketing and has learned from their mistakes—as a result, Excel offers a business plan to its Representatives that strives for simplicity and that is constantly reengineered to help people make some money as quickly as possible. It is one of the cheapest and most accessible ways for individuals and families, without capital or specialized knowledge, to build their own businesses.

The principal architect of what is known as the Excel opportunity is a man named Steve Smith. Founder Kenny Troutt will tell you that much of the credit for Excel's unique business approach and culture belongs to Steve.

Chasing a Dream

Sometimes good can come from bad. That's the way Steve Smith looks at the falling out he had with his father when he was 37 years old and working for his dad in the family paint manufacturing business in El Paso, Texas.

"I had never worked for anyone else except my father, and one day in 1982 we had an argument and I quit the business that day," Steve recalls. "It's funny because years later, we discussed why we didn't patch things up right away, and he said, 'Because I thought you were going to come back and talk to me and straighten things out.' And I told my father, 'I thought you were going to do that too!'"

Neither one did, so Steve found himself with a wife and two children to support and absolutely no idea about what he was going to do with his future. The Smith family relocated to Austin, Texas, where Steve started brokering paint products and looking for a foothold in business. "My problem was I had never really worked for anyone and didn't want to start. But I had no sense of direction."

It was a lousy time in Texas to try to find yourself, economically or otherwise. The 1983 oil bust brought many Texans to their knees financially, including Steve Smith. "We had no home and no car," Steve remembers. "A doctor friend of ours let us stay for free in a rental property he owned. When we had to get somewhere, we caught a ride from friends. It was a tough time."

One day, a friend told Steve about a way he could make "buckets of money." At that point, Steve was perhaps the easiest prospect in the world for such an appeal. "He showed me a plan and a video about relationship marketing," Steve told me. "Unlike many who are exposed to such a presentation for the first time, I thought this concept of relationship marketing was the most impressive thing I'd ever seen." He jumped right in, selling a line of health food and diet supplements. "But it seemed like about three minutes later, the company went out of business."

Steve Smith was back where he started—but not really, because for the first time he had grasped the power of network marketing. He couldn't get it out of his head. The wheels were turning.

"Then I came upon a company that was developing a network market plan for U.S. Sprint," Steve explains. "It made a lot of sense to me, because it seemed like the purest form of this business concept. Everyone could do a little work gathering customers for a product line that everyone needed and which enjoyed great credibility—telecommunications services. I decided this was the industry where I wanted to do network marketing. I couldn't see myself pushing diet pills."

With telephone deregulation just underway and network marketing of phone services still in its infancy, it was rough going for Steve and his family. He worked with a couple of communications firms but from his perspective still struggled to find financial traction and professional satisfaction.

In early 1988, Steve met Kenny Troutt. "You know what it's like when you meet someone the first time and you know instantly that this is a person you've just got to know better? That's the way it was for me when I met Kenny," Steve fondly recalls.

Steve's mission became to sell Kenny Troutt on the idea of using a network marketing approach in his fledgling Excel Communications. Steve still had a family to feed, however. "I was driving back to El Paso to visit my family—and hopefully borrow some money!—when I noticed those decorative strings of red chilies, called *ristras,* hanging on all the doors in West Texas. So I returned to Austin with a truckload of them, set up shop on the side of the road, and sold them all in half a day.

"So I went back for more, and before I knew it, I was selling them by the trailerfull. I cleared about $50,000 very quickly during the fall season of 1988. It was an interesting experience sitting in a truck on the side of the road developing Excel's original network marketing plan in between chili sales!"

By early 1989, Kenny and Steve were ready for blastoff—and that's exactly what happened. There was just one sobering catch for Steve, one he looks back on now with some glee: He was anticipating a huge corporate position and package. "Instead, Kenny looked at me with a kind of twinkle in his eye and told me, 'Steve, you've done such a great job convincing me that this plan can't fail—so that's how you're going to make *your* money!'"

And he did. "I barely had a penny to my name when I started," Steve says. "Not only did I hold meetings to recruit people where no one showed up, there was one I scheduled down in Houston where even the guy who was organizing it with me didn't show up!

"It wasn't easy, but the simplicity of our plan worked for me just like it's working for people today. I got my three Representatives, who started getting their [Representatives]. And from those three Representatives have sprung every one of the Reps and all of the customers in Excel today."

Today, Steve and his wife, Sarah, own two beautiful Texas ranches and their own helicopter. Steve Smith has become one of the legendary voices of network marketing, and his marketing genius is not only revered in Excel but is chronicled in journals like *Success* magazine.

The Power of Network Marketing

What makes the business approach that Steve Smith helped perfect for Excel so powerful and popular? Excel calls itself a *network marketing company*, because the Independent Representatives who rely heavily on personal contacts—their network of family members, friends, associates, and friends of friends and associates—use and sell the company's communications products and services, instead of the more traditional marketing efforts, such as advertising.

Excel can also be called a *multilevel marketing business* (the term is often used interchangeably with network marketing), since Representatives make money not only by selling Excel's products and services but by convincing others to do the same. "Upline" and "downline" business relationships determine the distribution of ongoing income—including commissions based on sales and bonuses paid on the basis of how good the Rep is at building a network of customers and customer gatherers.

Network marketers like to dramatize the income-generating power of their business approach by posing a simple question: Which would you rather have—a million dollars in cash right here right now, or a penny, the value of which will double every day for a month? Choosing the million dollars up front would, of course, cost you millions of dollars by the end of that month.

In the abstract, that's not a hard concept to grasp. Just do the math! Designing a real business plan to unlock network marketing's true power, however, drawing tens of thousands of enthusiastic recruits, was the tough task Kenny Troutt assigned to Steve Smith. By all accounts, the mission has been accomplished.

Sitting with Steve in an empty meeting room adjacent to an auditorium in which he is about to make a speech, I am struck by his calm, low-key manner—an interesting complement to the high-octane, high-energy Kenny Troutt. Sarah Smith warns me later not to be fooled by her husband's outward appearance. Inside, she says, is a fiercely competitive spirit and a relentless drive to win.

Still, the 50-year-old Smith is gracious and approachable, which is why his progress through any lobby where an Excel meeting is being held is painstakingly slow. "He'd stand there and talk to the Reps for hours if we didn't pull him away to keep to his schedule," an Excel staff member told me.

A few minutes into our conversation, during which I relate some of my background, Steve says, "It sounds like I could learn as much from you as you're trying to learn from me." I dismiss the suggestion out of hand, of course, but his expression of modesty quickly puts me at ease. There is a great deal of experience and wisdom to be mined from this man who has helped pave the way for tens of thousands of Americans to take part in the rebirth of one of our country's greatest traditions and most cherished dreams—being one's own boss.

Your Own Business— It's the Place to Be!

Across America, millions are embracing the challenge of starting their own businesses and are looking for the best way to do it. There are 22.1 million small businesses in the United States today, and they are the engine propelling the American economy. Small business owners represent half the American workforce and create two out of every three new jobs.

In a historical departure, women are creating new businesses at a faster rate than are men. A new word has even been coined in recognition of the growing number of working mothers leaving nine-to-five jobs for the flexibility, opportunity, and challenges of their own companies—they call themselves "mompreneurs"!

An increasing number of small businesses are ceasing to exist because they are becoming very big businesses. In an issue ranking its latest list of the 400 wealthiest Americans, *Forbes* magazine observes that great fortunes are being created almost monthly in the U.S. today by young entrepreneurs who didn't have a dime 10 or 15 years ago. There are 43 new people in the *Forbes* 400 class of 1996. That means nearly one in nine are newcomers in the last year. Kenny Troutt is one of them.

Since 1990, 238 new people have made it onto the list, displacing an equal number of others. For the most part, they are founding their fortunes on clever and inventive ideas and technologies, bearing out a forecast made by writer and economist George Gilder seven years ago that the 1990s would bring "a global economy dominated more and more by fortunes of thought rather than hoards of things."

The *Forbes* staff discovered this when it analyzed the fortunes of the *Forbes* 400: "In the not-so-distant past, wealth was almost always based on possession of physical assets. Wealth was timber, oil, real estate, factories or printing presses. Almost all of today's new fortunes are based not on hard assets but on ideas and organizing principles."

Yet, as Kenny Troutt has cautioned, the odds of achieving long-lasting success in the traditional world of small business are long: 85 percent close their doors in the first five years. Standard businesses that start with less than $10,000 in the bank are especially vulnerable.

Enter network marketing and the dramatic growth of the self-employed owners of home-based businesses. According to Link Resources, a prominent New York City–based market research firm, nearly 25 million home-based business owners are operating either full- or part-time. It is estimated that a new home-based business is started in the United States every 11 seconds. These businesses generate more than $382 billion in annual revenues and are responsible for creating more than 8,200 new jobs and entrepreneurial positions every day.

Many of these enterprises follow the direct selling or network marketing approaches. According to the Washington, D.C.–based Direct Selling Association, since 1990 alone, annual sales by direct selling companies have increased some 30 percent to $18 billion—51 percent of it through network marketing. The number of salespeople in these businesses has also grown by 30 percent to 7.2 million—58 percent of them network marketers.

Why such rapid growth? An article in *Inc.* magazine delineates the following advantages of the network marketing approach for entrepreneurs seeking their own business opportunities:

○ It eliminates the need for slick advertising.
○ In a world of marketing noise, friends and family are the only salespeople customers listen to and trust.
○ It reduces the cost of acquiring customers.
○ It reduces cash-flow risks, because merchandise has to sell before Representatives or distributors get paid.
○ It enables a company to build a large sales force very cheaply.
○ It capitalizes on the exploding supply of the self-employed, recently estimated by the *Los Angeles Times* to account for up to 15 percent of the American workforce.

Budding entrepreneurs of limited means choosing home-based opportunities over franchises and other approaches can find the risks and requirements lessened even more significantly in a network marketing business. *Entrepreneur* magazine itemizes a few of the things you *won't* have to do, such as these:

o You don't need to purchase equipment.
o You don't need to maintain and manage inventory.
o You don't need to apply for licenses or make tax deposits.
o You don't need to manage a marketing budget.
o You don't need to buy expensive insurance.
o You don't need to hire and pay a lawyer.
o You don't need to manage employees.
o You don't need to deal with government agencies.
o You don't need to apply for a bank loan.
o You don't need to obtain capital from investors.

Even big companies are getting into the act, though not all of them want to admit it, as *Inc.* magazine discovered:

From the top of *Inc.*'s 500 companies to the bottom are product and service companies that have adopted multilevel marketing to control overhead, create means of distribution, and build a national sales force on a budget. All of these companies have tapped into a growing contingent of displaced workers, professionals worried about their future, at-home moms and couples—all looking to get into business for themselves.

The Virtual Simplicity of Starting a Business

It has never been easier to start your own business. And the emergence of low-cost, simple-to-use communications and information technology is going to make it even easier while at the same time improving your odds of success.

Excel and companies like it—teamed up with accessible, user-friendly communications and information technology—have markedly improved the average person's chances for success as a business owner. More than ever before, it doesn't matter where you live or where you come from, whether you are restricted to your home due to disabilities or family responsibilities, or which language you speak—your territory stretches across America and could soon extend around the world.

You might call it your virtual business. For a few dollars, you can own and run your own company: a company without walls, a warehouse without inventory, a workplace without a workforce, a back room without billing or accounting, an asset without capital. The only thing that's real is the profit!

A senior executive at IBM recently observed that it is possible today to build and run a profitable multinational business from a home office equipped with a phone, a computer, a printer, and a modem. The biggest bookstore in the world, she noted, is not really a store at all. It's a virtual bookstore on a web site on the Internet that has a greater sales volume than a Barnes & Noble superstore!

What empowers today's entrepreneurs and puts so much business potential within their grasp is the speed at which new communications technologies are made available to the average person. Technology is becoming ever more complex in what it can do while at the same time becoming simpler to use and cheaper to buy.

Consider that the capacity of the microprocessor is doubling at a rate of every 15 to 18 months and will continue to do so for the foreseeable future. The IBM executive I spoke to illustrates the impact of this development by recalling that just 10 years ago she attempted to perform a particularly complex function on the largest mainframe computer her company had to offer—the kind of computer that used to fill an entire room—and "brought it to its knees"; today, she does the same function with ease on a "think pad" at her desk!

A recent article in *Success* magazine sums up the marriage of network marketing entrepreneurship and technology this way: "[multilevel marketing] is creating a whole new marketplace 'outside the box' of TV advertising, storefronts, inventory and middlemen, and has the power to render the conventional retail world obsolete. That power arises from the union of modern technology—computerized record keeping and telecommunications—with the ancient art of schmoozing."

This "union" has propelled Excel and the entire direct selling/network marketing industry into one of the hottest trends in the business world today. Around the world, 20 million work in the industry, not including China.

Richard Poe, a leading authority on network marketing, is so confident that direct selling and technology make a good combination that he sees it bringing on a whole new era of entrepreneurship, which he calls "Wave 3." In his best-selling book, *Wave 3: The New Era in Network Marketing,* Poe writes: "The most advanced network marketing companies today stress simplicity above all. They use computers, management systems, and cutting-edge telecommunications to make life as easy as possible for the average distributor."

John Fogg, editor of *Upline,* pinpoints the role technology can and should play in building a network marketing business when he observes: "All of the tools and technology free you up to focus on that one most intangible part of this business, which is relationships with people. Your job is to develop your people and support them in building their business."

Success in Network Marketing

Developing people and supporting them in their business—
Steve Smith understands well this most essential ingredient
in network marketing. "I've seen thousands of people start
their new Excel businesses over the last few years," he has
said. "All of them have had their own ideas about how to
best achieve success. Some believe that an immediate and
intensive advertising effort is the best way to start quickly.
Others subscribe to the philosophy that touring from city to
city is the fastest way to build a business.

"And there's nothing wrong with any of these ideas.
But just like in any other business, the best-laid plans
won't work unless you first have a solid understanding of
the fundamentals."

In Excel, like most network marketing businesses, the
essential ingredient of success is the business presentation. This is your sales pitch, the opportunity you create,
or are given, to convince your friends, relatives, coworkers, or total strangers to join your business. "The goal of
an Excel Representative is to build an organization of
customer gatherers. And although there are a number of
ways to go about it, all of them require a business presentation," says Steve. And while laying out the specifics of
the plan in a clear and accurate fashion is essential,
there's a more important mission.

"No prospect ever leaves a business presentation
remembering everything about our marketing plan,"

Smith advises. "But if you can make them remember how excited you were and how much fun you were having, you'll be successful.

"That's what people are looking for—something to be excited about, something that can produce a great income and be fun at the same time."

Excel's Stairway of Success

With chronically high rates of turnover among its practitioners, motivation is essential in network marketing. So is recognition. Excel has devised a system where people "promote themselves" and are rewarded accordingly every step of the way.

One of the most common myths about independent businesspeople is that they have gone out on their own to be alone. Yet, like most of us, those building their own businesses still seek and are motivated by recognition from their families, their peers, and the leaders of their industry.

Excel offers its Independent Representatives a series of steps on a "Stairway of Success." Climbing to higher levels brings increased financial rewards in the form of higher residuals and bonuses, not to mention the income potential from having an ever-greater network of down-line customers.

Just as important, attaining greater heights carries with it the respect and admiration of those you respect and admire: your friends, your family, members of your upline, your downline, and the Excel corporate leadership. Perhaps most important of all, excelling in Excel affords one the opportunity to be a mentor to hundreds of hopeful newcomers to the business and to develop close personal relationships with other successful people. Many of the Excel top performers I talked to cited this role and opportunity as among the most rewarding features of their new career.

How does one earn money and recognition from climbing Excel's Stairway of Success? Your fundamental goal is to sign up customers for Excel's communications services and convince others to do the same. These individuals become part of your downline. Your income is based on the following:

o   Commissions paid according to the volume of product used by your customers and those in your downline
o   An attractive schedule of leadership bonuses, which grow as you advance in the business, based on the number of customer-gathering people you successfully bring into Excel and the long distance customers they sign up

As outlined in chapter 1, it costs next to nothing to start. Signing up as an Independent Representative (IR) requires only a $50 fully refundable application fee. Most serious entrants in the business also purchase an optional Management Services program for $195, which provides them with all the initial training, information, and home office systems they need to get started. Individuals enrolling in this program are known as Managing Representatives (MRs).

From that point forward, the goal is to "promote yourself" to higher positions of sales leadership in the company. Should you attend an Excel business presentation, you will become acquainted with the specific requirements for each level as well as the compensation schedules and bonuses each level brings. Here, in a brief step by step, is the stairway Excel Representatives seek to climb:

Advanced Representative (AR) An Independent Representative who has successfully reached the first leadership level in Excel.

Qualified Representative (QR) An IR who has successfully qualified for all income from Excel's seven-level compensation plan (compensation is based on the long-distance calling activity of one's customers and customer's customers, to a certain depth).

Senior Representative (SR) An IR who is developing his or her leadership skills and who has successfully built the beginning framework of an Excel business.

Regional Director (RD) An IR who has attained a high level of organizational leadership and visibility. Responsibilities include promoting and conducting various organizational events as well as directing Area Coordinators (the role of Area Coordinators is discussed below).

Executive Director (ED)   Executive Directors have proven themselves to be individuals who can lead, motivate, and coordinate sales organizations.

Senior Director (SD)   Like the fabled Diamond level in the Amway business, the Senior Director position is where it's at in Excel. SDs have promoted themselves to the highest and most distinguished leadership position Excel offers. They are individuals who have succeeded in making their Excel business a full-time occupation.

Recognizing the importance of education and the fact that most people are poorly equipped with the training they need to be successful entrepreneurs, Excel also offers income opportunities for those who wish to emphasize this endeavor rather than build sales organizations and downlines.

Area Coordinator (AC)   This position is available to anyone interested in training Managing Representatives. Trainers are typically people who have a history of success, are good communicators and motivators, and have prepared themselves to understand and communicate the Excel program. Once qualified, they are paid based on the number of MRs they train.

Regional Training Director (RTD)   A regional director or non-IR Area Coordinator who has been in good standing for at least six months. The RTD trains Area Coordinators and Managing Representatives.

National Training Director (NTD)   After nine successful months, an RTD can be appointed to this post. NTDs train Area Coordinators, hold regularly scheduled training schools, and perform as Excel's primary field training leaders.

Surrounding Yourself with Success

Recognition comes in other ways at Excel. Since 1994, one of the highlights of the annual Excelebration meeting has been the moment at which 25 individuals, couples, or partners in the business are honored with the Circle of Excellence Award. The recipients are selected by a vote of Excelebration attendees based on "demonstrated excellence in professional relationships, teamwork, leadership, support and concern for persons in one's own and others' organizations, and a commitment to the Excel opportunity."

Kenny Troutt and Steve Smith also recognize outstanding Excel Representatives by naming them to the Eagle Team. Members of this team are typically top money earners and have reached the Executive Director or Senior Director level. Twenty-nine individuals, couples, or partners currently enjoy this high honor. You'll meet many of these successful entrepreneurs in ensuing chapters.

The best of the best are named Presidential Directors by Kenny and Steve. Together with the Eagle Team, they comprise Excel's Leadership Council. The council meets quarterly in Dallas with Kenny to discuss important business developments and new directions for the company. All of the six current Presidential Directors are top ten money earners and Senior Directors. They are Randy and Melissa Davis, Mike and Barbara Lammons, Russ and Mary Noland, Paul Orberson, Meg Kelly-Smith, and Al Thomas. Later, you'll learn more about each of them.

In addition, another Excel plus is the enriching experience of surrounding oneself with other successful people. Invitations to Steve and Sarah Smith's beautiful Cherry Springs Ranch in south-central Texas and barbecues at Kenny and Lisa Troutt's new mansion in Dallas tell you that you've arrived! But most agree that the greatest reward comes from watching the people you personally bring into the business realize their dreams and change their lives.

For most of Excel's top performers, the opportunity to meet other successful people and help others become successful are far more valuable than the monthly checks. They have not simply become rich through Excel, they have been *enriched.*

ANSWERING THE QUESTION WHY

AIDED BY CHARTS, an overhead projector, and slides, Steve Schulz moves through the explanation of the Excel business opportunity with efficiency and clarity. Many in the crowd take notes; others just listen intently. Steve's explanation seems so simple.

Then Steve puts down his pointer and pen and looks out at his audience. "I can teach you how, but I can't teach you why. What you have to do on your own is figure out the why."

After meeting and talking with dozens of Excel's most successful Representatives, I have discovered that the answers to the question "Why do this business?" are as varied and diverse as the people in the business.

Some have known little but misfortune their whole lives; others were sitting at the top of highly respected, professional careers. Some just wanted to make a little extra money to pay off a few bills; others were determined from the start to make millions. Some are high school and college dropouts; others have MBAs or law or medical degrees. Some joined to climb out of poverty; others joined because they were already making six-figure incomes but had no time to enjoy their affluence. Some signed up so they could do something together as a family; others did it to save their families. Some began as passionate believers in the power of network marketing; others believed these businesses were a sham but joined as a favor to the friend or family member who invited them in.

They have come to Excel from all backgrounds and circumstances, driven by different dreams—and they now share a journey together. With little in common but Excel, many have become good friends and as close as family. Having the opportunity to share a part of their lives with other successful people is clearly one of the greatest rewards that comes with climbing high in this business.

Seeking Another Rainbow

Excel Executive Director and corporate trainer Bob Torsey believes that the most common denominator among people joining the business is "the desire to do something different with their lives."

"People who are totally content with their lives don't often join Excel," he told me. "We attract those who for any of a number of reasons want to change what they're doing."

It's not a question of being a failure, Bob emphasizes. "We're also appealing to many highly successful people from all kinds of highly skilled professions," he explains. "They've found one rainbow. Now they're ready to seek another."

For years Bob was chasing his elusive rainbow in the corporate world. A vice president of marketing for a $500-million-plus building materials company, he was working 70 to 80 hours a week and was well paid for his efforts—until he became a victim of corporate downsizing.

Despite the rug being pulled from under him in the traditional business environment, Bob initially reacted to Excel with "arrogance and skepticism," he reports. "But then I met Kenny Troutt in December 1992, and I thought that he's either stark-raving mad or he's really going to do it. I decided I'm hitching my cart to that horse!"

Today, Bob maintains that his Excel business is more than just his downline: "I consider all of the Representatives I train to be a part of my business, regardless if they are a member of my downline or not. Their success is what makes the Excel opportunity so special to me." He credits his wife, Lois, with his success. "I couldn't have done it without her love and support," he says fondly. Frequently asked about his level of wealth, Bob replies in this telling fashion: "I live where I want to live. I drive what I want to drive. I pretty much come and go as I please. And I don't have all the pressure. So I guess I'm pretty wealthy!"

Recalling the daily grind of the corporate world, Bob sizes up the bottom line by saying, "I'd rather have another hour in my back pocket than another buck. I thank God daily for the Excel opportunity."

Others also find their goals changing as they climb higher in Excel. "I'm a big believer in goals," Steve Schulz says. At the outset, the goals he and his partner Pat Hintze set were mostly monetary. Having succeeded beyond their wildest dreams, Steve tells us, "Every New Year's Eve, Colleen and I and our three kids sit down as a family and ask ourselves, What do we want to get out of this business in the coming year? What are our goals?"

Last New Year's Eve, two of the couple's little girls had some very specific goals in mind. Their four-year-old said, "Every time you or Mommy go somewhere, we have to go with you." The six-year-old said, "Disney World!"

Now Steve and Colleen schedule presentations and appearances around the school calendar so the family can travel together as much as possible (and, yes, one of those trips took the Schulzes to Disney World). For

Steve, the answer to the question why is, "So we can do this as a big-time family affair."

Doing It for the Freedom

Paul Orberson's goal seemed ambitious at the time. For thirteen years he had taught school and coached basketball and football, earning an annual salary of $35,000 for his efforts. He hoped he could match that in Excel, and it seemed like a crazy idea.

"I went to an Excel business presentation in November of 1990 and decided to get in. Within six months, I went full-time," Paul says. "It wasn't really the money I was after. The reason I got in it in the first place was for the freedom. If, in the process, I could match what I made in teaching, I thought that would be great."

Within just a few years, Paul had not only done that, but he was making six figures a month, every month. "It feels real good!" Paul says. Today, he is Excel's top money earner and a millionaire many times over.

Yet, sitting across from this down-to-earth, denim-clad 40-year-old, you could easily mistake him for just another guy next door. "Success hasn't changed me as a person. It still isn't the money. Money will never make you happy, but neither will being broke."

What accounts for Paul's success? "I took the attitude that people like me and you—average people—can do anything if we put our minds to it. You see, we're not paid for what we do; we're paid for what we start. I decided to pay a price and start this business to build a legacy for my family and for generations to come.

"I didn't know anything about telecommunications. I didn't like to speak in public. I didn't have any contacts. But I was afraid that I would never have an opportunity like this again. It's not just an opportunity of a lifetime, it's the opportunity of ten lifetimes!"

Given his prior career, Paul Orberson knows the priceless value of a good coach and a wise teacher. When I ask him where he sees the business headed in the future, he answers bluntly, "Jim, I have no idea. But I have confidence in Kenny Troutt. He's the most committed person to what he's doing that I've ever seen in my life. When he says he's going to build the largest communications company in the world, then I know he's going to do it. Kenny Troutt and Steve Smith took an interest in me and believed in me. That's what gave me the confidence to succeed."

He could be the guy sitting next to you in a diner or the fellow waiting in line in front of you at the hardware store. Nothing in Paul Orberson's words, appearance, or demeanor would indicate his status as one of the country's most successful network marketers. Except one thing: he's a bundle of nervous energy. "I can't sit still even for five minutes," he confesses. Paul is earnest and straightforward in his approach to both conversation and business, shunning high-minded concepts and modestly fending off my repeated efforts to get him to draw deeper significance from his achievements.

To Paul, success seems like a simple equation—not easy, but simple. Kenny and Steve developed the perfect business for average people like Paul. Paul learned from them, placed his trust in them, and grabbed hold of the opportunity and worked it as hard as he could. Now, this typical working man makes money even when he's not working, freeing himself from the time-for-money trade-off that has snared so many of us.

Paul Orberson may be a man of few modest words when talking about himself, but his inspiring—and some would say unlikely—success speaks volumes for thousands of Excel Representatives who draw hope from his example.

Locking the Doors to the Past

Rick Ricketts and his wife, Brenda, are two people who were inspired by Paul Orberson's success. Rick spent twenty-three years in the furniture business, which he considered a safe, substantial bet compared to "risky" multilevel business schemes. Then, without warning, a road construction project blocked off the parking lot in front of the store. "It killed my business," Rick told me.

"Brenda saw the potential of Excel before I did," Rick recalls. "All I could see was the $100 bonuses I could get for bringing people in. Then, on July 18,

1994, Brenda and I were listening to Paul Orberson speak. After Paul said 'ain't' for the fourth time, Brenda leaned over and poked me in the ribs and said, 'I think you can do this business too!'

"You see, I thought I owned three stores, but in fact they owned me. I have a high school education. I didn't think I had a lot of options. We got in part-time at first while our business limped along. But we promised ourselves that if we could just make $6,000 a month, we'd leave that behind. After just four months, we got a check for $5,987. That was close enough, so I locked the doors on my business."

The Ricketts were first introduced to Excel "by a 23-year-old college kid who did us the favor of a lifetime" and were later inspired onward by Paul Orberson, a former basketball coach who said "ain't" a few too many times. Once chained to his desk managing three stores, today Rick Ricketts has rediscovered family life and never ceases to marvel that "you can even not be there and your income still goes up!"

"You Wouldn't Believe How Much Money I'm Making!"

Once Mike Lammons starts talking about Excel, there's just no stopping him.

"People look at a crazy guy like me and figure if I can do it, so can they," Mike tells me, trying to explain how he and wife Barbara climbed all the way to the number two position among Excel's top money earners in less than three years.

Today, Mike and Barbara manage their Excel customer and representative organization, estimated at more than 35,000 Representatives and 185,000 customers, from their home in Fresno, California. Their roots are readily apparent from Mike's Texas twang and Barbara's leftover trace of a Mississippi drawl. "We met in Texas, when I was working at a gas station," Mike recalls. "I liked to say that I was in the oil business two quarts deep!"

Migrating to California, the Lammonses moved in and out of various small business opportunities, finally building a successful health club business. Yet, the ever-restless Mike—who likes to burn off excess energy riding his motorcycle throughout the Southwest—tired of the daily grind of the health club. "We sold our business and I basically retired," Mike says. "I was a 50-year-old guy with no dreams and no vision for the future."

One day in March 1993, the Lammonses did something they had never done before: they answered a want ad in the newspaper. The ad invited people to an Excel business presentation. Against what they thought was their better judgment, the Lammonses decided to check it out. "It was the hokiest thing I ever saw," Mike remembers. "We were one of just two couples there in this big hotel room—and the other couple walked out. I had never heard of Excel and I wasn't about to fork over

$195 to sign up. So I left on a motorcycle trip and left Barbara with the decision."

Given Mike's negativism, it's a good thing he went on his trip. By the time he had reached his destination (boat races in Phoenix), Barbara had signed them up. "I thought it was a crossroads for us," she says.

"I called Mike in Phoenix, and he knew right away," she recalls. "He said, 'You did it, didn't you?' and I told him I had." Today, a grateful Mike says, "Barbara saw something in this business I couldn't see at first. I've had to eat a lot of crow!"

Mike's first goal was to simply get his money back. The two will never forget the thrill of their very first $100 check. "Kenny Troutt asked us later what's the most exciting thing that has ever happened to us in this business, and we told him it was that very first check."

From the beginning, Mike has developed a standard reply when the curious inquire about his Excel income. "I've told everyone the same thing from the very beginning, whether I was making a few dollars or hundreds of thousands: 'You wouldn't believe how much money I'm making in this business!'"

It's a fitting response, given the skepticism that the Lammonses find when they pitch Excel to prospects. "Many begin with the belief that there is no money to be made, and even if there were, they wouldn't be successful at it. That's why I tell people they wouldn't believe how much money I make."

The Lammonses believe that it's the high volume of rejections that pose the greatest risk to the new Excel Representative. "We come from a business background, and that has helped us a great deal," Mike says. "And I've got a very thick skin. I'll pitch the business and the products to anyone, anywhere, anytime. Cold-calling doesn't bother me like it does so many others."

Even though the Excel strategy attempts to soften the blow of rejection by advising Reps to focus on family members and friends, Mike says that can be a double-edged sword. "I've seen many people actually get turned down by their loved ones, and it can be more devastating than being rejected by strangers. It's happened to me! My mother and two brothers are still not my customers, and I've had some close friends make me really mad by turning me down," Mike says.

The Lammonses also advise people in the business to adopt a sensible strategy that builds on their strengths and minimizes their weaknesses. "I have a friend who owned five restaurants. He told me he made a lot of money but he had no freedom. I wasn't working at anything except Excel, and so I said, 'That's great— because all I have is freedom. We'd make a great team.' So Barbara and I hold meetings and present the business plan for people like him. That takes the pressure off those who don't like to speak in public or have no time to present the plan." Mike's friend has since sold his restaurants and works the business full-time as an Executive Director.

In most network marketing businesses, it's the depth of one's organization that counts. The Lammonses have personally sponsored just thirty-two people in the "front line" of their business. "Twenty-one have never done anything," Mike explains. "The other eleven got a few people into the business—but six among them really saw their businesses take off based on the strength of those they brought into it. It's those six Executive Directors that really helped build the success Barbara and I have enjoyed."

The lesson: "It didn't matter whether we recruited wide, as long as we recruited deep."

Today, the Lammonses work hard at their business, but according to Barbara, "It's the fun of Excel that keeps us going, and it's a wonderful feeling to see people we help make a few hundred dollars a month, if that is their goal, or even help them change their lives."

When I call the Lammonses to ask some follow-up questions, I catch them both relaxing at home at 12:00 noon on a weekday. "I'm just sitting around here in my Bermuda shorts," Mike tells me.

"Good for you! I'm sitting here in my office in a blue suit," I reply. I ask Mike to describe a typical week.

"I conduct three or four meetings a week," he tells me, "and travel on behalf of my organization about 10 to 14 days a month. I'm busy, but I keep my own schedule and I have fun. You've got to have fun!"

I try once more to find out just how much Mike gets paid to have all that fun. His reply again is, "Jim, you wouldn't believe how much money I'm making!"

A Triple Play

News that your wife is about to have triplets can force you to focus on the family budget, not to mention that most precious of commodities called time—very fast! That's what happened to Scott Pospichal of Jupiter, Florida, the day he and wife Janet visited her obstetrician for an ultrasound. "Great news!" their doctor told them. "Your baby's heartbeat sounds strong and healthy." The Pospichals joyfully embraced.

"Oops—what's that?" the doctor continued. "It's another heartbeat. Twins!" The happy parents-to-be gulped once and embraced again. "Wait a second. There's a third. Congratulations, you're going to have triplets!" The Pospichals sat immobilized, half expecting the doctor to keep on going with more such wonderful news. But he stopped at three, and today Scott and Janet are the proud and happy parents of three beautiful little girls and a five-year-old son, Jason.

The happy but life-altering turn of events made Scott all the more thankful that he had found Excel.

He was about as unlikely a candidate for the business as one could imagine. "I was coaching basketball at Palm Beach Community College in Florida," Scott told me. "That's what I always wanted to do. My dream was fulfilled."

Nonetheless, at the urging of the college president, Scott started building an Excel business. He was good at it from the start. "I matched my coaching income after four months. I tripled it in six months. But I couldn't give up coaching. It was hard to walk away from."

The Pospichals became convinced to make a complete break when Scott contracted a serious case of chicken pox—for adults, still a dangerous disease. He was at home, not working and not doing much of anything. "But the Excel checks kept rolling in. It was then I learned about the kind of security residual income can bring." Using a favorite phrase among Excel's high achievers, Scott reports it was then that "I fired my job." At the time he quit his coaching job, Scott was pulling in more than $23,000 a month.

All the Pospichals can think of as they gaze down upon their three baby daughters is how they could ever have given them the life they deserve were it not for the Excel opportunity.

An Average Joe

Despite being just 33 years old and already one of Excel's top ten money earners, Phillip Wells describes himself as an average guy. "I grew up two hours south of Little Rock and worked in a gas station to put myself through college," Phillip told me. After school, he meandered to Southern Arkansas, putting in a stint as an assistant manager with Wal-Mart and working in various sales jobs. After opening his own business in Wichita, Kansas, Phillip moved to Tulsa, where he was introduced to Excel. "Excel caught my eye, and within five months I had shut my five-year-old business and was working Excel full-time."

It wasn't easy. "The first six months were very tough," Phillip recalls. "But Paul Orberson was a great inspiration for me and still is! Pretty soon, things picked up. I started making $10,000 a month in Excel, but then I hit a plateau."

Most successful Excel people aren't content living life on the plateaus—they're looking for new peaks to climb. Phillip is no exception. "We made a video and it really helped my business take off. I think it's because people could relate to someone like me. I'm just an average Joe."

Within a year of making the video and two and a half years in Excel, Phillip had reached the number six position of Excel top money earners. Talking to him, I get the sense that it's just another plateau. Phillip Wells won't be there very long!

Equal Opportunity

Chuck and Sandra Hoover of Houston, Texas, weren't looking to set the world on fire when they started their Excel business. They were simply average, working Americans who wanted a fair chance to adequately provide for their family and build some financial security.

Creating one of the first organizations in Excel, the Hoovers have been working the business for eight years and are among the company's top ten money earners.

Talking to them, one can sense their quiet pride in such an achievement.

The couple married right out of high school. "We were childhood sweethearts," Chuck says. "And after thirty years of marriage, we're still going strong."

Hard work came easy to the Hoovers—in both the financial services business and in auto sales. "We always felt a strong moral obligation to put food on the table for our four children. What really made Excel different was that it allowed us to build a business that was totally our own. But even more important, Excel offers more of a level playing field than any business I've ever seen. I've seen doctors and lawyers give up their practices for this company. Everyone has the same opportunity to succeed regardless of background or level of education." It's that reassurance that the American dream and sense of fair play are still alive and well that seems to satisfy Chuck the most. "Excel has allowed us to go through life with dignity," he says.

Sandy's focus is also on the dignity she can help bring to others. "Everyone else's goals have become ours. In Excel, we get the chance to help others realize their dreams too, as we are advancing our own. That's one of the best rewards you can ever have in life."

Model of Success

When Larry Bowditch was growing up in Kingsport, Tennessee, he wanted to be a research chemist. Boyhood dreams die hard, but as he got older, Larry realized he loved being around people, and while research chemistry has done great things for humanity, it's not what one would call a "people" business.

So the goalposts moved, and Larry—coming from a family of limited means—struggled to put himself through college. "Unfortunately, my money ran out after about a year and a half," Larry remembers. So he wandered through various jobs, winding up as an inspector for a glass company in Huntsville, Alabama. That's where he met and married Lucille.

As Larry continued his search for the perfect job and struggled (unsuccessfully) to save enough money to go back to college, the couple settled in Garland, Texas, just outside of Dallas. In 1983, Larry landed a job with IBM. It was a good job, but a demanding one. Lucille brought in extra money working as a receptionist while she raised the couple's four sons.

"I learned a lot at IBM: marketing, customer support, training skills," Larry told me.

"But he was never home!" Lucille chimes in.

"What we both aspired to," says Larry, "was harmony between our work, social, and spiritual lives. I thought about going into social work. The problem is, it's hard to leave one career field, go into another, and start at the same income level you had."

"There was definitely something wrong with this picture," Lucille agrees.

One day, a coworker of Larry's, named Kern Johnson, introduced him to Excel and his upline sponsor, Lee

Lemons. "They just saw me coming. I was ripe for this business," Larry says with a laugh, referring to his job burnout and strong desire to work with people. "The simplicity was beautiful. They told me there was a way to make money when other people made long-distance phone calls—and the path to success was helping others succeed."

Lucille brought her own invaluable asset to the table: a vast network of people to potentially bring into the business. She went full-time almost at once. "I liked the idea that I could set my own schedule and talk with all the people I knew," she recalls.

Meanwhile, downsizing was proceeding with full force in corporate America and especially at IBM. The frequent voluntary separation offers began looking increasingly attractive to Larry. Lee Lemons urged him to proceed with caution. "That tells you a lot about both Lee and Excel. Sometimes these network marketing businesses overpromise. They promise you the moon tomorrow. Not this one," Larry observes.

Finally, however, he could resist no longer. Another buyout offer came in November 1993, and this time, Larry says, "I was ready. I was really ready!" He got six months of separation pay to live on while he worked Excel with Lucille full-time. Within nine months, they met and passed their previous income.

Today, the Bowditches are Excel Executive Directors and National Training Directors. They work at home as a team, which is a wonderful lifestyle change for Lucille.

"All the time Larry was in IBM, I couldn't relate to what he was doing. Now, after twenty-one years of marriage, we're finally living our lives together," says Lucille.

"Our goals are to help people change their lives and achieve their dreams," Larry observes. "It makes me sad when I see people trapped in corporate America, like I was, or locked into making minimum wage."

As successful African-American entrepreneurs, Larry and Lucille have reflected thoughtfully on the example they set in their community. "If I have one message to African-Americans, it's the same one I'd share with everybody, and that is: Keep an open mind. Don't assume that everything's a scam and a rip-off. Don't be so negative. Other opportunities may have been closed to you, but Excel is open to everyone.

"This is the kind of job where no resume is required!"

As we'll see in the next chapter, that kind of opportunity is a rare find, given the tough, insecure economic climate of the 1990s.

INDEPENDENCE DAY

THE COLD WAR is over. America is at peace. The economy is growing solidly in all regions of the country, and the experts say we are at full employment. With interest rates low and inflation in check, corporate profits are up and the stock market is in the stratosphere.

Are we simply riding high atop the business cycle, soon to be headed for a fall? Not likely. Despite some ups and downs, this party has been going on for a long, long time.

Economist and *Newsweek* columnist Robert J. Samuelson explains that "by most objective standards, the last half century in our national life has been enormously successful. Americans have achieved unprecedented levels of material prosperity and personal freedom. We are healthier, work at less exhausting jobs, and live longer than any time in our history."

Yet a quiet desperation has taken hold in the minds and spirits of millions of families and communities. The statistics tell us we should be buoyant and that our future is overflowing with possibility. But something's wrong. Something's missing.

Perhaps it's the feeling that we're not really in control of our lives, that our time belongs to someone else, that we're working harder and longer to build opportunity for our families—and that even after a lifetime of commitment to that goal, our security could be pulled out from under us at any time. One middle manager working for a big oil company put it this way after being dismissed after 25 years with his company: "They can call it reengineering, downsizing, restructuring, but it still means you're fired."

The What, Me Worry? Economy

Despite the happy face economic statistics, many Americans are worried about their income security. They're beginning to realize that they've bought homes and cars they can't afford, delayed any serious savings plans, and overextended themselves in both work and debt. Call it the morning after to the What, Me Worry? economy. Consider these recent findings:

○ A University of Wisconsin study cited by *Business
Week* found that even though stories about corporate downsizing have faded from the front
pages in recent months, both actual layoffs and
fear of layoffs are up in 1997 over 1996. Many
new jobs are created in place of the ones that are
lost, but just three-quarters of downsized employees land a new position within three years. Those
who do find a new position also find their pay
reduced by an average of 14 percent.

○ Labor Department statistics show that since
1979 more than 36 million jobs were eliminated.
The *New York Times* puts the figure at closer
to 43 million.

○ In one-third of all households, a family member
has lost a job and nearly 40 percent more know
of a relative, friend, or neighbor who has been
laid off.

○ One in 10 adults in America say that a lost job in
their household had precipitated a major crisis in
their lives.

○ In a role reversal from earlier times, workers with
at least some college education make up the
majority of people whose jobs were eliminated.
Better-paid workers (those making at least
$50,000 per year) account for twice the share
of lost jobs than they did in the 1980s.

○ Just a few examples of casualty counts of the
1990s: 123,000 lost jobs at AT&T; 18,800 lost

jobs at Delta Airlines; 16,800 lost jobs at East-
man Kodak.

○ In the last 12 months alone—during a time
when corporate profits and stock prices have
skyrocketed—Best Products cut 10,000 jobs,
Aetna Life cut 8,200, Sunbeam cut 6,000,
Wells Fargo Bank lost 3,800, and Apple
Computer squeezed out 4,100.

The fear is spreading, and it's eating away at many
Americans' optimism and sense of dignity. When *USA
Today* asked baby boomers between the ages of 32 and
50 to write to the newspaper about the security of their
white-collar professional jobs, the responses included
poignant and often bitter tales of lost self-respect, broken marriages, and even suicide. One reader sadly
chronicled the decline of his once-neighborly suburban
community:

A bunker mentality has replaced neighborhood fel-
lowship. A nomadic existence has usurped the concept of roots—of living in one place for a lifetime.
The security that comes from stability is what baby
boomers want most. And it is the very thing that
today seems so hard to possess.

If jobs are more likely to disappear than ever before,
they also pay less. Over the last 15 years, average weekly
earnings dropped 17 percent in construction, 16 percent
in transportation, 7 percent in manufacturing, and 22

percent in retail jobs. Overall, real wages have declined 12 percent while worker productivity has increased 24 percent.

Shrunken expectations have poisoned the culture of many workplaces. Seventy-five percent say companies are less loyal to employees than they were 10 years ago. And 70 percent say most working people compete more with their coworkers than they cooperate.

It's not surprising that when it comes to work and income security, many Americans on Main Street are not sharing in the euphoria in evidence on Wall Street. There's a disconnection that many are struggling to comprehend. We live in a time of booming business but diminishing dreams.

That explains why the *New York Times* found in a recent survey that two-thirds of American families were scaling back their spending due to concerns about their economic security. One-fifth said they had imposed severe cuts on their budgets. More have expected to be much better off now than they actually are.

More than just imaginary insecurities are at stake here. Samuelson believes that, ironically, decades of overall economic progress have fueled unreasonable demands for proliferate public spending. He describes the post–World War II period as an "Age of Entitlement"—a heady, optimistic era in which both genuine economic growth and an overpromising government inflated our expectations and instilled within many of us a debilitating dependence on public largesse.

"In 1929, government spending accounted for about 11 percent of the nation's economic output," Samuelson tells us. "Three percent for the federal government, the rest for states, counties, and municipalities. By 1990, this share had risen to about 38 percent, nearly two-thirds of it federal."

Not surprisingly, the engines propelling this great American entitlement machine are quickly running out of gas. Beginning in the 1970s, the federal government began to run up huge deficits. Despite an improving deficit situation in the mid-1990s, by 1996 total federal debt stood at $5.1 trillion, requiring an interest payment that swallowed up 15 percent of the federal budget that year—$241 billion!

The impending retrenchment (some would even predict collapse) of government's entitlement machine—from student loans to health care to retirement checks—has darkened our outlook, while soaring prices have placed many of the essentials of the American dream out of reach for many families. For every American who fears losing his or her job, there are probably many more who wonder why it now takes two incomes to secure the same quality of life formerly provided by one.

- o Nearly 60 percent of women now work outside of the home. About 70 percent of women with children under 18 years of age are working, up from 45 percent just 20 years ago.
- o The average new car costs $20,000.

○ Home prices have soared more than 70 percent over the last decade.

○ By one estimate, in 10 years we'll have to earn a salary 80 percent higher than it is today just to keep pace with higher costs.

○ It's going to cost at least $123,000 to put a child born this year through four years at a public university when he or she reaches college age.

○ People who haven't saved and have no stream of business or investment income should be prepared to live on the current maximum monthly Social Security payment of just $1,248 a month.

Taking Control Again

Freedom. It's arguably the most beautiful word in the English language—or any language. It means different things to different people and cultures, but the exhilaration that comes from being in control of one's own destiny is universal. A common thread running through the reflections of the most successful people in Excel was that the business set them free from the strings, demands, and insecurities of today's economy.

In the darkest days of the Great Depression, as the storm clouds of an impending global war were gathering on the horizon, President Franklin Delano Roosevelt spoke often and eloquently about not only the freedom from want but also the freedom from fear.

The distinction is critical and illuminates the dilemma for many in the 1990s. Our society has achieved freedom from want—indeed, most of us enjoy a level of material prosperity other societies and eras never thought possible. But we live with the growing fear that our prosperity is illusory. Prosperity demands more of our time to be maintained, and neither increasing our level of education nor working longer or harder offers any guarantee that it won't disappear virtually overnight.

Suppose you were offered a path out of this "splendid wilderness"? What if there was a business where you could promote yourself? A business where the only boss who could lay you off was you? Suppose there was a business where the way to get ahead was not to make yourself look good at others' expense but to help others perform well and succeed?

Many believe they have found such a business.

Flying High Again

Jordan Adler, an Eagle Team member from Tempe, Arizona, surveyed the constant ups and downs of the airline industry and decided to hedge his bets. As a corporate trainer for America West Airlines, he watched the regional carrier's boom years quickly go bust during the Persian Gulf War and the economic slowdown that followed.

"America West was laying people off," Jordan told me. "I wasn't downsized, but I thought I might be. So I thought, why not give Excel a try? Maybe earn some extra dollars, pay off some debts, and have something to do just in case."

Jordan set modest goals at first, building his Excel business during lunch hours and evenings. "I really had no idea what would happen. After three and a half years, I found myself among Excel's top 100 money earners."

The greatest reward can't be measured in dollars and cents. "I decided when to leave my corporate job. No one decided for me," Jordan says with great satisfaction. "My dream always was to have a home in the mountains. I have that now—in the national forest in Pine, Arizona."

The daily grind of his past profession is a distant memory. Jordan now estimates he works about 20 hours a week. "Someone asked me to describe a typical day," he told me. "I couldn't do it. Every day is different."

Jordan Adler, now earning more money than he ever imagined and enjoying the recognition that comes from his peers and Excel leaders, relaxes in his dream home in the forests of Arizona and contemplates what he calls the paradox of Excel. "What brings people into this business—a personal desire to improve one's life—will not allow them to be successful. In order to be successful, one must focus on the goals and successes of others in order to achieve personal success."

Escaping the Poverty of Time

Focusing on others and helping them through troubling times was nothing new to Excel Executive Directors Rick and Cindy Brake, of Louisville, Kentucky. Rick was a mental health therapist in private practice and Cindy was a nurse.

"We got into Excel five years ago to make some residual income," Rick remembers. "Within two years, I was making more in a month from Excel than I made all year in the medical profession. Excel gave me the freedom I've been looking for all my life: the freedom to try new things, the freedom of time, and freedom from financial worry."

It's been a team effort all the way. "We built it together," says Cindy. "We work as partners, growing and adjusting along the way. Excel has definitely enhanced our relationship."

Most important of all, Rick emphasizes, "Excel has given us hope—and we, in turn, are able to give others hope. By changing our own lives, we're able to help others change their lives for the better."

No Experience Required

The leaders of Excel bring many skills from their former professions to their new business. They were teachers, coaches, doctors, real estate agents, small business owners, corporate executives, and homemakers. In the eyes of Senior Directors and Eagle Team members Kenny and Linda Gilmore, of Brandon, Mississippi, these skills can be helpful, but only one qualification is really required: you've got to love people and understand the people business.

"I spent 18 years in real estate and another 12 years in insurance," Kenny told me. "Then a friend told me about Excel and the plan Kenny Troutt had set up. All you have to do to make serious money in Excel is to show people the opportunity and teach them how to teach others to do the same. Four months after Linda and I started, we went full-time, and it's given us a lot more quality family time.

"The most important thing to understand about this business is that it's a people business. If you like people, you'll make it!"

Hopping on the Freedom Train

"I help people hop on the freedom train. That's what I do!" Excel Executive Director Beth Hinson draws her chair closer to me. Her eyes are alive and on fire. "I grew up in a small town in South Carolina that had all of two traffic lights," she said. "I was a single mom trying to support my family, and I didn't do very well. I sold fire extinguishers door-to-door and then trailer lots."

One day, her son called her and told her about a new business opportunity. "I was so excited, I wrote a check for the MR/AC position that I couldn't cover. But I was sick and tired of being broke, and by then I had a baby one-and-a-half years old to support. I told myself, I've got to make some changes!"

Today, Beth Hinson is one of Excel's top 13 money earners, and she doesn't mind anyone knowing where she came from or about all the counts against her. "I could quit right now and live off the residual income for the rest of my life," she says. "I'm finally free. But I can't and I won't. We're on a mission to help people like me who want something to change their lives. We haven't even scratched the surface!"

Moving Ahead of the Curve

Pat Hintze looked at the course of his father's life and decided it wasn't very good. "I was a sales representative for a paper company, slowly climbing my way up the ranks," he told me. "My dad did the same thing in his company, and I watched him get downsized after 22 years of hard work, with no pension plan to speak of. That scared me."

So with his wife, Cindy, along with boyhood friend and partner Steve Schulz and his wife, Colleen, Pat began to look for that special business that would give him financial freedom and the time he wanted to spend with his family. When Pat heard about Excel, he knew that he had finally found it. As he had so many other times in his life, the first thing he wanted to do was share his excitement with Steve.

"Pat called me at 10:30 on a Sunday night," Steve recalls. "He said, 'What are you and Colleen doing right now?' Both of us were teaching school at the time and our days started early. I said, 'What do you think we're doing? We're getting ready to go to sleep!' Pat was persistent. He told me he just had to come over and show me this business."

Pat Hintze did just that, and Steve knew right away they had found a winner.

"Our original goal was to make $203 per month, because that was our car payment. I thought we might get a free car out of this thing. I never for a moment thought Excel would become our principal source of income," Steve says.

Today, Pat and Steve, with Cindy and Colleen at their sides, are partners in the Excel business, ranking among the company's top earners and most sought-after teachers and motivators. The partners have thought long and hard about what makes Excel so successful and why they're so confident about the future. Says Steve, "We remember when this company was nothing more than four employees working in 900 square feet. Kenny Troutt and Steve Smith have really made it grow. They always seem to be six months ahead of the curve."

Says Pat, "It's the simplicity and the customer loyalty. I know my mom will always be my customer. No matter what the new products are, I'll take her and all my other personal customers out of the market!"

A Six-Figure Guy

Making six figures a year was really no big deal to David Jennings. What drove him to Excel was the raw deal he thought he was getting from the corporate world.

"I worked as a vice president for an oil company for 16 years," Dave told me. "I was a six-figure guy, but every time the oil business changed, my commission structure changed. I wanted out. I looked at franchises and at one point almost bought a dry cleaning business.

When I got into Excel 33 months ago, I went all out. Most important, I didn't want my wife to have to go back to work. Instead, Karen is now very active in the business with me. I've never been in a network marketing company prior to this—and I'll never be in another, because I'll never leave Excel."

David Jenning's decision to leave the oil business for Excel mirrors Kenny Troutt's decision to do the same a decade ago. David's success in both endeavors underscores the reality that there is no shortage of ways for smart people to make money in today's economy. In increasing numbers, however, those even at the highest levels of income and skill are demanding more than just short-term monetary compensation. Like David, they are looking for an endeavor where there are no limits to how much they can make, where they can set their own schedule and better balance work obligations with other priorities, such as family, and where they can establish a secure stream of income into the future, so that they continue to get paid even when they're not working.

Excel epitomizes an important development in network marketing: a greater focus on services rather than products. This, in turn, has attracted top professionals

Kenny Troutt,
3 years old, with brother
Terry, 1 year old.

Kenny Troutt (#1), 10 years old.

Kenny Troutt,
15 years old.

Kenny Troutt, 18 years old.

Kenny Troutt, Lisa Troutt, Sarah Smith, and Steve Smith at the Bootscootin' Barbecue on the grounds of corporate headquarters during Excelebration 1993.

Kenny Troutt and Steve Smith on the corporate jet.

Presidential Director Al Thomas receives the Circle of Excellence Award from Kenny Troutt at Excelebration 1994.

Photo courtesy of Andy De Stena

Presidential Directors Barbara and Michael Lammons with Kenny Troutt at Excelebration 1995.

Presidential Directors Russ and Mary Noland and Meg Kelly-Smith lead the Presidential Directors into Excelebration 1995.

Kenny Troutt and Steve Smith present the Circle of Excellence Award to Executive Director Pat Hintze at Excelebration 1995.

Jack McLaine, Lisa Troutt, Kenny Troutt, Catherine Kinney, and NYSE President William Johnston overlooking the floor of the NYSE the moment the ECI ticker registers on the board on May 10, 1996.

Catherine Kinney presents Kenny Troutt and Jack McLaine with Excel's certificate of listing on the NYSE on May 10, 1996.

Sarah Smith, Steve Smith, Kenny Troutt, and Lisa Troutt at Excelebration 1996.

Photo courtesy of Sal Sessa

Presidential Director
Paul Orberson at
Excelebration 1996.

Presidential Directors Melissa and
Randy Davis at Excelebration 1996.

Photo courtesy of Andy De Stena

One of Excel's original
handwritten downline
reports.

Lisa Troutt and Sarah Smith at Excelebration 1996.

Kenny Troutt receives the Ernst & Young Entrepreneur of the Year Award in the Emerging Company Category. Seated (left to right): Tammy Jacobs, Lisa Troutt, Sarah Smith, Susan Casner, and Tammy McLaine. Standing (left to right): Pete Wittmann, Kenny Troutt, Linda Martignon, Dan Martignon, Steve Smith, Bill Casner, and Jack McLaine.

Excel headquarters in Dallas, Texas.

from many fields who have never before been considered likely candidates for network marketing.

Getting Paid for a Lifetime

"I spent 17 years in corporate America," says John Jones. "I was a senior account manager for General DataCom. My wife, Patrice, worked for a local phone company. We both felt like prisoners. What I was really looking for was something I could do on my own. One day, I became totally stressed out at work. I knew it was time to get out."

Out of the blue, an old college friend whom John hadn't spoken to in 10 years looked him up and introduced him to a business called Excel. "As hungry as I was for something new," John says, "Patrice and I were highly skeptical. We really checked up on it before getting in. Thanks to her background in the telephone business, Patrice was able to determine that the New York market was wide open for us."

Just 17 months later, John quit his job and went into the business full-time; Patrice quit her job and joined him just three months after that. Today, four years after John's stress attack, the Joneses have reached the pivotal position of Senior Director. Now they are watching friend after friend from their discarded corporate lives join them in the business.

John offers this insight: "You need certain qualities to succeed in this business—a vision of where you want to go, hustle, faith, and patience, so you can get paid for a lifetime!"

Sometimes a Million Isn't Enough

Russ and Mary Noland were doing very well before they had ever heard of Excel. "We were both realtors in Houston and we were closing over a million dollars in sales monthly," Russ told me. "But we were working seven days a week to do it. We had a great lifestyle, but we had no life."

Mary readily agrees. "We were very successful, but we had real estate burnout." The Nolands were ripe for a friendly takeover. "By the nature of our profession, we were meeting and networking with a lot of people, so we were always being dragged to different multilevel marketing meetings and presentations."

So what prompted the couple to trade in a profession in which they were selling more than $2 million in product a month for a business that both describe as very tough in its formative days? "When we got into Excel nearly seven years ago, Mary continued with real estate for a while," Russ says. "We wanted to get a life. We also saw how much money was flowing into telecommunications. That money's got to flow somewhere. In companies like AT&T, it flows to Wall Street. In Excel, it flows to Y'all Street!"

In a world eerily devoid of heroes, the Nolands, who are one of the six Excel Presidential Directors, are sure they have found one. "The greatest thing about Excel is the people," Mary says. "It may sound corny, but Kenny Troutt is our hero."

This Is Not Your Parent's Multilevel

One of the most common mistakes people make when assessing the network marketing industry and companies like Excel is in thinking it's a business for losers and housewives. That assessment is not only unfair to home-makers and those who have come upon hard times, it is also wrong. As evidenced by the examples of the Jennings, the Joneses, the Nolands, and others, Excel is also attracting many highly skilled professionals who soared to the top of their chosen fields only to find that the lifestyle it brought them was inadequate.

Take Dr. Michael Thompson, for example. He spent 11 years as a chiropractor, building one of the most successful practices in the state of Alabama. "I didn't need the money, and I simply wasn't interested in Excel," he told me. The interest might never have come were it not for the persistence of a friend, who was turned down by Michael seven times. "Finally, after he had driven seven hours and come into my waiting room with no appointment to talk to me about Excel, I gave him the grand sum of 20 minutes to persuade me," recalls Michael.

Because of his persistent friend and the fact that for all his success Michael realized he was not debt-free and had little time for himself, he began building the business. "I started doing business presentations after hours, and within six months, at age 36, I sold my practice." What excites Michael most is that he was not only able to change his own life, "but help others succeed too. That's a great reward to me."

It's a reward that many others in medical services careers are seeking as well. Their instinct to help people already burns strongly inside them. That's why they became doctors, nurses, and other medical services providers. "A lot of people in my group are refugees from health care and from the stress, the liability, the burnout, and the accountant's mentality that has come to characterize the practice of medicine today. They are drawn to Excel because it is streamlined, it is high-tech, and there are no products. And you have an even better opportunity to help people."

More Money or More Time?

It's been seven years since Kevin and Doreen Pine, of Hillsborough, California, were first drawn to Excel. Kevin had a successful dental practice and a teaching position at the University of California School of Dentistry. "In dentistry, you can have more money or you can have more time. In Excel, you don't have to make that choice. I can't say enough good things about it."

Kevin is amused when newcomers to the business express concern, asking if it's too late or if the business is saturated. "I point out that AT&T has about 55 to

60 percent of the market and we have about 3 percent. That doesn't sound like saturation to me! Whenever I'm asked when is the best time to get into Excel, I say, 'Right now!' I've been saying that for the last seven years, and I've been right every time."

Dirt under the Fingernails

Excel can bring together, under the same banner of success, skilled medical professionals like Dr. Michael Thompson and Dr. Kevin Pine and hard-working non-professionals like J. R. and Betty Scott, from Lee's Summit, Missouri, who proudly proclaim, "We've got dirt under our fingernails!"

"We're proof anyone can do this," J. R. told me. The Scotts have been married for 32 years and raised two kids. "It was a struggle, but we always paid our bills. There are people who have more degrees than a thermometer who haven't been able to do that."

Betty recalls, "We've done it all. J. R. sold insurance, worked as a highway engineer, and he even drove a truck. Then we got a degree from Hamburger U. and we managed a McDonald's. To make all that happen, we had to refinance our house."

Nearly four years ago, they were introduced to the Excel opportunity. In just four months, they matched their monthly income. Within a year, they crossed the six-figure per year mark. "There's people out there like us—you could call them hard-working, blue-collar people—who think they have no options. We're proof that it's not true. It just takes time and perseverance."

Nothing Succeeds Like Success

Lee Lemons, of Desoto, Texas, is proof that you don't have to hate your life to join this business. There is no "failures only need apply" sign hanging on Excel's front door. Many of the company's most successful Representatives don't dismiss or downgrade their previously acquired skills; they simply channel them towards new, more powerful personal goals.

Lee was a 13-year veteran of IBM, and in the course of that experience acquired top marketing skills and strong self-confidence. That's why when Lee was ready to jump into Excel, he did so, both feet first, in one big leap. For a time, Lee's wife, Rhonda, continued to work in accounting, duplicating a familiar pattern for two-income families making the transition to a network marketing business: one spouse maintains a stable, steady income while the other spouse builds the new business full-time.

It was rough going at first, recalls Lee, a thoughtful, soft-spoken man. "It took us 30 days to recruit our first Rep," he remembers. "I finally convinced this guy from India to join, but he misunderstood me and sent a check for $3.95 instead of $395!"

Lee and Rhonda established modest goals at first. "My initial goal was simply to get my money back," Lee says. "Then, we thought maybe this will be a good source of supplemental income, maybe a couple thousand a month. Once we achieved that, we moved the bar higher yet again, hoping to make $5,000 a month."

As the couple moved up the income ladder, other goals took center stage. "What I was really after was to be able to come home and take care of my kids," Rhonda says. "The most important thing about Excel to me is that we're doing things together as a family. And even when we're on vacation, we're still making money!"

Today Lee and Rhonda work the business exclusively and together as Senior Directors. They still get a kick out of the fact that while many Excel Reps in the early stages cite the goal of making a car payment as their initial income target, the Lemons family actually won the whole car, all at once, in a company contest.

What advice does this successful couple have for those just starting out? "I'm a big believer in training," Lee says. "People have to be properly trained. You have to keep it simple, and you have to work at it really hard. We have an expression that says, 'more meetings [to present the Excel business plan to prospects] mean more money,' and it's really true. Be committed, be persistent, and have faith in yourself."

Firing Yourself

Presidential Director Al Thomas is a favorite on the Excel speaking circuit, and it doesn't take long to understand why. He mixes common sense and humor (often at his own expense) to raise people's comfort level with the business. That's critical, for within an organization like Excel, one is constantly surrounded by successful, highly motivated people. For those still trying to make that leap to financial independence, it's an inspiring environment, but it can also be somewhat intimidating.

In his own humorous, irreverent way, Al puts people at ease. "The beautiful thing about this business," he tells them, "is if you have an unpleasant day or you mess something up, you can fire yourself. And then the next day you rehire yourself!" To Al, that's the opposite of what he found in real estate, the profession he pursued for 18 years in Sacramento and the Bay Area of Northern California. "The problem is that every time you sold a house, you were unemployed again."

Looking for the kind of freedom that month-after-month residual income could bring, Al joined Excel more than six years ago, and for the last four years he has devoted himself full-time to the business. "This business will work for anyone if you'll work the business," Al says in reassuring tones. It's not a get-rich-quick scheme. It takes hard work, determination, persistence, and a burning desire."

It's easy to understand why a man like Al Thomas has achieved a top ranking within Excel. Within five minutes of meeting him, he's talking to you as if he is your close friend. When I point out that we both had lived in

Sacramento, Al quickly rattles off names of people we might know in common. Sure enough, he finds a few. Several minutes later, he has me convinced that we have already met.

I ask him what guidance he has to offer to others coming into the business. "Prepare yourself for rejection," he quickly replies. "You'll get rejected a lot."

He adds, "My goal when I'm mentoring people in this business is to bring them out of their shells. Most people fear public speaking, and they fear rejection even more. Sometimes we have our people wear buttons referencing Excel so that they can be approached by interested parties instead of the other way around. Most important, I tell them about all the times I have been rejected. It still happens to this day! My downlines think, if those bad things can happen to Al, they can happen to us and we can still be successful."

Al's network marketing strategy is to "go wide fast," meaning one should gather plenty of Representatives as quickly as possible in order to increase the odds of bringing the few real stars into one's organization. "But the fact is, 80 percent of those you bring in won't do very much. You just have to face that fact. The remaining 20 percent will be more active, and among those you'll hopefully find 5 percent who will be the real leaders."

As a bachelor, Al enjoys the frequent travel and the many friends Excel has brought him all over the country. "Money is just a way to keep score in the business world.

What really counts is to be able to travel to a city to make a presentation, arrive earlier, meet up with some friends, play golf, and relax," he says. "I can afford to stay in great hotels, but more often than not my friends invite me to stay with them. It's a great feeling."

Freed from the often impersonal and insecure environment of the professional world, with all its accompanying pressures and time demands, Al Thomas, like many others in Excel, now celebrates Independence Day 365 days a year.

REMEMBERING
WHAT'S IMPORTANT

I OVERCAME CANCER TWICE. After the second time, I told myself, if I can do that, I can do anything. It helped me figure out what was really important," says Excel Presidential Director Melissa Davis.

November 1 is an important date in the lives of Randy and Melissa Davis, of Simpsonville, Kentucky. They married on November 1, 1991, joined Excel exactly one year later, and celebrated their second anniversary with Randy leaving his job as an alcohol and drug abuse counselor to devote his full time to building the couple's business.

It seems so neat and simple now, but it almost didn't happen.

"I went into Excel just about as skeptical as a person could be," Randy told me. When a friend urged him to come to a presentation on the Excel opportunity, Randy invoked the timeless excuse: "I don't have time." To be polite, he finally agreed to try to come to a meeting. Then he didn't show up. Apologies flowed. "I'll try to come next time," Randy said.

Second time—didn't show up. Third and fourth time—didn't show up. His friend's persistence, admirable in retrospect, became a pain in the, uh, neck. "I started turning on my answering machine so I could screen my calls," he says.

Randy eventually became more open-minded, especially after he and Melissa finally went and heard the presentation. "Randy's job was such that he was working about two days a week and playing a lot of golf," she recalls with a touch of envy. Melissa had a management job in a hospital. "He had the spare time, not me."

Randy and Melissa may have had different work patterns, but they shared a common love of spending—deficit spending!

"We've always been dreamers," Melissa says. "The problem was, our dreams were always larger than our income. We had debts. Lots of debts." They started checking out options—franchises, a sandwich shop, the real estate business—but each required either capital or savings to live off of for the short and medium term. No deal. For six weeks, the couple made excuses to miss the Excel presentation and ducked their friend's phone calls, but during that time a powerful feeling came over them, and it wouldn't go away. "What if this is the chance we've been praying for?" they wondered.

So the Davises finally decided to give Excel a chance, but even on their way over to the presentation they were still uncertain and skeptical. "We protected ourselves by embracing small goals at first. If Excel could help us pay a few bills, that would be just fine," Randy recalls. "When we really let ourselves go, we dreamed about having a house on the beach in Florida. It always seemed so out of reach."

Looking back on his skepticism, Randy is not surprised. "Eighty percent of first graders have high self-esteem," he explains. "By the time those first graders get to junior high, only 10 percent feel that way. In their senior year, 99 percent of those kids feel inferior. We're brought up in a system that tears us down. We're not conditioned to believe we can be successful. We're trained to be employees."

If Randy has reached his conclusions with a rationality one can't argue with, Melissa has reached them spiritually with a sincerity no one can doubt.

"I know the doctors would probably disagree, but somehow I believe my illnesses sprung from being unhappy and not fulfilling my dreams," she says. "I took all the courage I mustered to fight cancer and applied it to this business.

"I live life with a passion now. Excel's a passion with me. Driving down the street in my Mercedes with the top down and the wind blowing through my hair, I think how blessed I am to be here and to have found Excel. My advice to others is simple: Take this opportunity! Take it seriously. Grab it and run with it just as hard and as fast as you can!"

The Davises work the business together, and sometimes they work from their beach house in Florida!

America's Crisis in Values

Economically, the country may be strong—at least according to the statistics. But who would deny that our society is adrift when it comes to values? Most careers focus on a simple financial transaction: you give a company your time; they give you money back. Increasingly, however, Americans are finding that network marketing opportunities like Excel help them address not only monetary needs but personal and societal concerns as well.

Clearly, the traditional American family is in trouble. The signs are all around us:

○ Since 1970, there has been a 548 percent increase in the number of unmarried couples with children under 16 years of age.
○ In 1993, 31 percent of all babies were born to unwed mothers. In 1970, the ratio was 10.7 percent, and in 1950, it was just 3.9 percent.

o   There are nearly eight million single-parent
    households with children at home.

Many women have entered the workplace out of
necessity, and many others have pursued career aspirations. These are laudable motivations, but the impact on
children of both single-parent households and those in
which both spouses work outside the home is unmistak-
able. Denied the close supervision and careful nurturing of
times past, many children are drawn into or are victims of
destructive behavior. The most troubling trends include
drugs and alcohol, crime, and child abuse and neglect.

Drugs and Alcohol   According to a study conducted by the University of Michigan and the National
Institute on Drug Abuse, this nation's secondary school
students and young adults show a level of involvement
with illicit drugs that is greater than has even been docu-
mented in any other industrialized nation in the world.

o   Since 1991, the proportion of eighth graders tak-
    ing any illicit drug in the past 12 months has
    almost doubled, from 11 percent to 21 percent.
o   Since 1991, the proportion of tenth graders
    taking those drugs has risen by two-thirds,
    from 20 percent to 33 percent.
o   The proportion of twelfth graders taking any
    illicit drugs in the past 12 months has increased
    from 27 percent to 39 percent.

○ No substance is abused by youth more than alcohol, mirroring the nation as a whole. Some 15 million Americans are alcoholics, with alcohol abuse being responsible for approximately 100,000 deaths per year.

Crime A rise in youth crime, especially violent crime, stands out as a glaring exception to an otherwise improving public safety picture in the United States.

○ More than 1.5 million young people under age 18 were arrested for crimes in 1994.
○ Seventeen percent of all violent crimes are committed by young men under the age of 18.
○ The number of these crimes jumped 10 percent in a single year.

Child Abuse and Neglect Consider the following statistics:

○ In 1994, the last year for which complete figures are available, more than one million children were victims of abuse or neglect.
○ Reports of alleged mistreatment involving more than 2.9 million children were filed, an increase from 2.6 million in 1990.
○ Since 1990, more than 5,400 children have died as a result of abuse or neglect.

Family science researchers are finding disturbing links between the lack of parental involvement with children and those children's proclivity to problem behavior and learning disorders.

"Parents are right to be concerned about the squeeze on family time," the *Washington Post* concluded in a recent in-depth report. "Specialists say that children benefit intellectually and socially when the whole family is together—by listening to adult conversation, learning to relate to siblings and getting a clearer sense of the family's moral values."

A recent study by Search Institute, an organization specializing in research on children, examined 270,000 sixth to twelfth graders in 600 communities nationwide and discovered, according to the *Post,* that "children who spent at least four evenings a week at home with their families and had frequent, in-depth conversations with their parents were less likely to have sex and use alcohol or drugs."

The *Post* report also cited another study that taped dinner conversations between parents and children in the Boston area for eight years and uncovered this interesting result: "Preschoolers who were exposed to mealtime discussions among parents and siblings did better on vocabulary and reading tests in elementary school than those who weren't.

"The conversations expanded the children's vocabulary and improved their ability to tell a story or give an explanation. . . ."

Many busy parents, intuitively aware of research findings like these, have made well-intentioned efforts to reserve so-called quality time with their children. But further research is showing that the notion of parents scheduling their children as if they were just another entry on their appointment calendars doesn't work and misses the point.

A recent *Newsweek* cover story on the growing impact of the lack of daily parental involvement in children's lives reported the following:

> Experts say that many of the most important elements in children's lives—regular routines and domestic rituals, consistency, the sense that their parents know and care about them—are exactly what's jettisoned when quality time substitutes for quantity time. . . . Parents who race in the door at 7:30 P.M. and head straight for the fax machine are making it perfectly clear where their loyalties lie, and the kids are showing the scars.

Teachers are reporting an increasing number of discipline problems with kids, which they attribute to the lack of time and attention from parents.

The dilemma and concern appear particularly troublesome for working women. "I *think* she's doing okay," one working mother told *Newsweek* about her young daughter. "If it were up to me, I'd spend more time with her. I wish I were able to stay home, but that's just not possible."

Eager to aid the family finances, pursue career aspirations, and raise a family all at once, many women attempt to carry a near-impossible burden. While *Newsweek* found that men are picking up a greater share of child-rearing and household responsibilities, the burden still falls most heavily on women, whether or not they are also working outside the home.

New research cited by *Newsweek* found that women employed outside the home devote an average of 6.6 hours to the most essential, child-care responsibilities, such as bathing, feeding, reading, and playing. The average employed man devotes just 2.5 hours to those activities. For women remaining in the home, the average time doubles to more than 12 hours per week. For an unemployed man at home, the amount of time stays essentially unchanged.

None of these figures includes the many more hours spent on housekeeping, shopping, laundry, cooking, and other errands. When married couples working outside the home were asked how such duties were divided between the spouses, the response "We share it 50-50" was the response of 43 percent of the men but only 19 percent of the women. Could someone be fibbing? To the wives in that survey, their husbands' responses might conjure up the famous expression of comedian Will Rogers: "Who are you going to believe—me or your own eyes?"

Alongside its documentation of a serious problem, *Newsweek*'s offering of the most common solutions is despairingly sparse. We are told to slow down, seek reduced work schedules for reduced pay, and be more faithful to routines important to children, such as meals and reading bedtime stories. At best, those are Band-Aid approaches.

A Better Approach

Today, tens of thousands of parents—men and women—have discovered a better approach: they build their own low-cost Excel businesses at home, allowing one and later two parents to set their own schedules, earn serious, long-term residual income, and put family first.

It's all part of remembering what's really important—and it's something that Larry Cheatham, of Bowling Green, Kentucky, never forgot. He dreamed of the day that his wife could break out of those statistics. Larry was a high school teacher and coach, while Bonnie worked as a secretary in the school. "I began in Excel four years ago because I was looking for a way to make a few extra dollars and maybe pay for a new car," Larry remembers. "But with three children, my real dream was to get my wife home."

That dream was fulfilled! Within a year, the Cheathams, now Eagle Team members, were making more in their Excel business than their combined salaries at the school. Now, not only is Bonnie a full-time mom, but Larry is a full-time dad!

Ask Steve Walker, of Spokane, Washington, what he does, and he'll proudly tell you, "I'm a stay-at-home dad!" Steve has accomplished this because he and his wife, Roberta, have built a successful Excel business, and one thing above all others keeps them focused and totally committed to it. "We get to raise our own kids," Roberta says.

"This country has run amok over the last 20 years," Steve believes. "We've got to get back to some basic family values. We've got day care centers, not parents, raising our kids."

Steve reflects on the strange experience of playing outside in the neighborhood with his children on weekday afternoons and seeing no other children around. "One day, my son asked me where all the other kids were," Steve recalls. "I told him that they were all in day care. And he looked up at me and said, 'I want to be with you, Dad.'"

For stay-at-home parents Steve and Roberta Walker, no greater reward from any business or profession could possible match that special moment.

The Living Proof

Loren Friedman lives life with a passion. Maybe it's because he's lucky to be alive. Loren knew the American dream even before he was introduced to Excel. He grew up in a working-class family, the son of a roofer. With the loving support of his family, Loren became a corporate attorney and landed a good job in New York City.

Then he was struck by a devastating illness. "My large intestine basically exploded," he told me. "I had four operations, and the surgeons told me later they never thought I'd survive."

The near-death experience prompted Loren to take stock of life. So did the fact that Loren and his wife, Vicki, were destroyed financially. "My wife worked as a secretary in a hotel. I wanted to get her out of there, but I didn't want to go back to practicing law."

Introduced to Excel, Loren's skeptical lawyer's mind threw up all kinds of roadblocks. "It didn't impress me at all at first. But then I studied what was going on in telecommunications and the Information Superhighway, and I realized this wasn't about peddling some tacky product. This was a hot industry that I wanted to be a part of. I just decided I wanted to be a toll collector on the Information Superhighway rather than a toll payer."

Loren borrowed the money to fly to Dallas, where he met Kenny Troutt. "I owe him everything. I've hitched my wagon to his star," he says. Within five months, the Friedmans' Excel business was producing more in one month than Vicki was making all year in the hotel. "So I sent her a dozen roses with a card that said "Dreams do come true." That was the last day she ever worked for someone else.

The Friedmans' advice is to "keep it simple." Loren loves to talk about what he calls his "$195 Jaguar," with the $195 representing all it took to get into a business opportunity that has produced so much. He also has a boat, which he named *The Living Proof.* Loren Friedman sure is living proof that you can live the American dream—twice!

Life on the Double

John Gergen, of Eagan, Minnesota, was doing what most Minnesotans were doing one Sunday afternoon two and a half years ago: he was watching the Vikings play football on TV. Right in the middle of the game, John's wife, Alice, got another phone call from her brother. "If you hand me that phone, we're divorced," John told her. He knew his brother-in-law was calling to pitch one of those multilevel marketing schemes. "I wasn't interested. I'd seen them all before," John says.

However, there's something about caring for newborn twins that can cause you to reexamine your life real fast! "The babies came 10 weeks early," John remembers with a smile. "And 10 weeks later, we started our Excel business. It wasn't a question of money. We made enough in our real estate business. It was a question of time. When you're working 90 hours a week, there's not enough time for the family. We did it to stay home."

Today, the Gergens are Senior Directors in Excel, and their time is their own. "This is the best business in America today. It's the McDonald's of network marketing. It's unbelievable!"

Pulling Together

It's during times of tragedy and adversity when the true character of a business and the people in it are really tested. It's when you find out whether a company is really a family or just another heartless corporation. The story of Jay Smith and his wife, Meg Kelly-Smith, provided just such a test for Excel.

As a woman executive, Meg had a lot to be proud of. In the 1980s, she broke through barriers cleared by few women before her. By 1988, she was a senior vice president of the twelfth largest savings and loan in America, which had a $12 billion loan portfolio and hundreds of employees. She was at the zenith of a successful 22-year career in banking.

There was just one problem. "My job was in San Diego in Southern California and I was married to a guy who owned a large insurance services business in Marin County, north of San Francisco," Meg told me. That guy was Jay Smith. "I did my best to commute by air between San Francisco and San Diego, but by 1988 we were both so busy we hardly saw each other."

Meg and Jay decided it was time for a major change. "We wanted something we could build together, with residual income, something we could do as equals. We were looking for the perfect business, and we found it in Excel," Meg says. The Smiths went full-time right away. To Meg, the uniqueness of the company was that "it eliminated everything having to do with products and inventory. The fact that it's so easily duplicable is the key."

The year 1990, when the Smiths started their Excel business, may not seem that long ago on the calendar, but it's light-years away for the company, for those were the days of infancy. "I remember when there were three full-time employees, a few desks facing each other, and virtually no materials," Meg reflects.

Reaching their own financial goals faster than they ever expected, Jay Smith focused on training and became one of the most revered teachers and motivators in the business. The reason was simple, remembers a grateful Randy Davis: "Jay's philosophy was that by helping everyone, whether in his organization or not, he would help the company. By helping the company, he would automatically help himself. He would encourage everyone he met to do the same thing. He was a person of the highest character and values I've ever met."

Jay Smith was at the airport on his way to an Excel meeting in 1995. He never made it. Jay blacked out due to a heart ailment, fell, and died of a head injury. It was a devastating loss for Meg, of course, but also for the entire Excel family. That family has closed ranks around Meg, helping her through with immeasurable love and support. Jay's memory has been honored by the establishment of the Jay Smith Excellence in Training Award, perhaps the company's most revered honor.

Randy and Melissa Davis were the first recipients, in 1995. "It's probably the most special award I've ever received," Randy observes. "Not just because of my relationship with Jay, but because it tells me that the tradition Jay started, his legacy of instruction, is continuing. Hopefully I can make the difference in someone's life the way he did in mine."

One year later, at Excelebration '96 in Dallas, Meg Kelly-Smith presented the second annual award to Senior Director Pat Hintze, to whom Jay had offered countless hours of guidance and inspiration. It was an emotional moment. "I have mixed emotions, because I knew Jay for so long. He helped us when we were struggling," says Pat.

Meg continues to bestow her love for Jay, by nurturing and growing the business they built together and by teaching others with skill and insight to do the same.

Never Too Busy to Care

It was an unexpected gift of flowers that revealed the true character of Excel to Senior Directors Mark and Cindy Pentecost, from Caledonia, Michigan.

Mark taught high school math and coached basketball for 16 years, while Cindy managed the household. "Like so many others, when I first heard about Excel I kept saying I was too busy. It finally took my mom and dad to make me sit down and take a serious look at this business," Mark recalls.

The Pentecosts' goals in Excel were typically modest at first: "We thought it would be useful to pay off some credit cards. But in just one year I was making more in a month at Excel than my entire annual salary at the high school," Mark told me.

"In teaching, I got paid the same whether I was the best teacher in the school or the worst. In Excel, you get paid according to what you put into it. It's a different way to keep score." Cindy echoes Mark's enthusiasm: "What you really get is the freedom of time. Mark was one of the only dads at our kids' softball games. Within 12 months, we were debt-free."

"We got into this business to change our lives, but we quickly found an even greater and more rewarding opportunity, and that's to change other people's lives, too," Cindy says.

The money, the time, the independence, the freedom to help others—Mark and Cindy count the blessings they received from their Excel business over and over. The real test came when tragedy struck the Pentecost family. Their two daughters were in a serious car accident, and one girl suffered critical brain injuries. The family kept a three-month, day-and-night vigil by her side as she began a slow recovery.

They will never forget a special gesture from Kenny Troutt and Steve Smith shortly after the devastating accident. With her voice shaking, Cindy tells me: "Somehow Kenny found out what had happened, found out where we were, and sent us flowers. We just started crying again. To me that says everything about the business we're in."

A Family Affair

Brothers Bob and Phil Mims have taken Excel's concept of family being the most loyal customer to the next logical step: they have become business partners too! Bob and his wife, Ali, live in Vancouver, Washington. Phil and Lucie live some 2,000 miles away in Southlake, Texas. Together, the couples run one of Excel's most vital business partnerships, falling within the ranks of the top ten money earners.

An experienced pilot, Bob Mims used to fly corporate jets. "It was a good profession, and I made plenty of money. Being the pilot convinced me that no matter what I did, I wanted to be the guy in the cockpit. I couldn't see myself in the back of the plane."

When Bob's brother, Phil, began building an Excel business after 17 years in the wholesale jewelry business, he was instantly drawn to the company as the alternative he'd been looking for. "Three years ago, I closed my jewelry business," Phil told me. "Bob quit flying. We're proof that a partnership approach can work well in Excel."

What excites Phil the most about Excel are not the past achievements but those yet to come. "We've had all this success, and we haven't even scratched the surface. There's growth, new products, the international arena—they're all just sitting out there.

"I'm absolutely convinced that Kenny Troutt will do just what he says and build the largest communications company in the world. He'll take a whole lot of millionaires with him."

IT'S NOT TOO LATE

AVE AND ELLEN Funk spent years working around the clock building businesses. "The only problem was," Dave says wryly, "is that as employees we were building those businesses for someone else."

One day, Dave answered an ad for corporate trainers. It was an Excel ad. He was immediately excited about the opportunity. "Right away, I thought this could be our ticket," Dave says.

Ellen was skeptical, however. Before the couple moved to Dallas, she and Dave had both grown up in conservative rural Iowa on small farms near small towns. "I thought people like us didn't do this," she said. "I couldn't understand why Dave was writing a check for training materials when we couldn't even pay our credit card bills."

Still, the Funks spent every minute they could working their new business while hanging on to their jobs. Their bosses weren't very happy with the diversion of the Funks' time, attention, and energy. "Finally, we were both fired, and you know what? I felt like a giant elephant had been lifted off my shoulders," Dave says.

That was October 1992. Today, the couple is straddling age 50 and earning a six-figure income at their own pace. "We can't afford to go to work anymore!" Dave likes to joke. "When we found Excel, we found a secure retirement. And I'm not just talking about the money. We're also having fun and making a lot of friends."

As for Ellen, she was finally convinced that Excel was more than just a sideline activity. "When I saw the checks, that convinced me that this business is for real."

The Funks believe that the future of Excel rests with Americans 40 to 60 years of age like themselves, who are finally starting to worry about retirement and being financially secure in their later years. "They should be worried," Dave observes. He sadly relates the story of a friend back in Iowa who worked at a company for 25 years. He was nearing retirement but was downsized out of a job and left with a $200-a-month pension to live on. "He is 66 years old now but looks 80," Dave says quietly.

Spending Like
There's No Tomorrow

"I can't think about that today. I'll think about that tomorrow." For years, millions of now-middle-aged adults belonging to the so-called baby boom generation have been taking the same approach to retirement and savings that Scarlett O'Hara took whenever she was in a jam in *Gone with the Wind.*

As a group, Americans born in the post-war boom years—those coming of age in the turbulent sixties and the "me decade" of the seventies and living high on the hog in the eighties and nineties—are woefully ill-prepared for retirement. We're living longer than ever before with lifestyles more extravagant than ever before. What's going to happen when the job is over, the income dries up, the savings are gone, and one's health falters? As the first boomers cross the 50-year threshold, many are starting to ask those questions for the first time in their lives.

Social Security and Medicare:
Countdown to Insolvency

Perhaps you're one of those planning to rely upon the nation's two massive entitlement programs, into which you have been paying ever-increasing amounts your entire working life. You'd better think twice. The programs are going broke, and the politicians in Washington have found neither the political will nor consensus to do anything about it. Here's why and how it's happening.

Started in 1935, Social Security worked reasonably well for the first half century of its existence. That's because there were many more workers paying in than there were retirees pulling money out, not to mention the fact that the initial retirement age of 65 actually exceeded a male's life expectancy at the time.

Over time, the ratio of workers to retirees has shrunk dramatically. In 1950, there were 16 workers for every Social Security beneficiary. In 1960, the ratio had narrowed to 5 to 1. Today, the ratio is 3 to 1, and by the year 2030, it will be 2 to 1. It will be as if each two-income couple will have an extra "parent" to take care of, in addition to their own.

Thanks to so many boomers in the workforce, not to mention a long string of payroll tax increases, for the next 15 years or so, the Social Security trust fund will continue to build up a surplus. Then, from about 2012 to 2019, as baby boomers retire, spending for benefits will exceed payroll taxes coming in. Interest income earned on the current surplus will make up the difference for a while. From 2019 to 2029, the fund will start redeeming its bonds for cash to make payments. By the year 2029, exactly one century after the stock market crash that signaled the onslaught of the Great Depression, Social Security will become insolvent. At that time, one in every five Americans will be age 65 or older. If you're around 35 years of age today, you'll be one of them—and your life expectancy will be pushing 80!

While the burdens on the system grow ever greater, the dependency is getting stronger. According to the most recent figures available:

- For 63 percent of beneficiaries, Social Security provides at least 50 percent of their total income.
- For 26 percent, it provides 90 percent of total income.
- For 14 percent, Social Security is their only source of income.

Seniors are worried, and so are soon-to-be seniors. A 1995 poll conducted by the American Association of Retired Persons (AARP) found that 55 percent of Americans agreed with this statement: "In theory, Social Security is still a good idea, but I doubt if this country can afford it anymore." Baby boomers are the most skeptical; only 16 percent expressed confidence in the viability of the system.

Those expecting to join the 37 million seniors and others who depend on the Medicare program to care for them during illness should also reflect carefully on what's happening to that program.

In 1996, Medicare gobbled up $199 billion, about 12 percent of the total federal budget. Expenses have exceeded receipts since 1995, and they are still going up as health care costs rise and the elderly live longer.

The most immediate problem is that the trust fund that finances inpatient hospital care under Medicare Part A is projected to spend its last nickel in the year 2001.

The long-term structural problem facing Medicare is similar to that faced by Social Security: over the next 30 years, as baby boomers start to retire in droves, fewer taxpayers will be financing the benefits of more senior citizens. In 1995, there were 3.9 workers paying taxes to cover each Medicare beneficiary. The Medicare trustees estimate that by 2030 there will be just 2.2 workers for every beneficiary. So in addition to that extra "parent" the working couple of the future will be paying for, they will also be caring for an anonymous sick relative!

Even if politicians find the will to fix Social Security and Medicare, what will that fix entail? What kind of retirement lifestyle will it buy for you? The current maximum Social Security benefit is only about $1,248 a month. For many Americans, especially spendthrift boomers, that will buy just a fraction of the lifestyle to which they've grown accustomed. Instead of redeeming frequent flyer miles for first-class air tickets and luxury resort vacations, legions of us will be learning to clip grocery store coupons for the first time in our lives.

This fact alone could significantly delay retirement for many Americans now entering middle age. "They won't be able to retire at 55 or even at 65, because of inadequate savings, reduced employer benefits, and the likely scaling back of what the federal government will provide," the *Wall Street Journal* reported recently.

The age at which you can receive maximum Social Security retirement benefits is already scheduled to be pushed back over time, from 65 to 67. Ever-greater portions of those benefits are likely to be taxed. And as discussed, the benefits themselves are in question because of the looming insolvency of the program.

Economist Paul Craig Roberts spells it out bluntly in a recent issue of *Business Week:*

> The two government programs underwriting an aging population—Medicare and Social Security—are both in financial trouble. According to the 1995 Social Security Trustees Report, retirees face—unless there are substantial increases in the payroll tax—a 10 percent reduction in hospital and retirement benefits by the year 2010, a 27 percent reduction by 2020, and a 41 percent reduction by 2040.

Finding Security with Excel

Retirement should be a time of security, with opportunities to travel, spend time with grandchildren, and do the things you've always wanted to do after a lifetime of hard work. Increasingly, both government and employers are incapable of providing security or opportunities for older Americans. The only way it can be done is to continually take more from the children in the form of greater payroll taxes or reductions in investments and education. What parent or grandparent wants to do that?

The leaders of Excel suggest there is a better way, and no matter what your age or past spending habits, they insist it's not too late!

The Shock of Their Lives

Despite early success in Excel, Daryl and Betty Hallmark, of Hopkinsville, Kentucky, couldn't bring themselves to give up their teaching jobs to build their Excel business full-time. Then they checked out how much they would receive in teaching retirement. "We both resigned the next month," says Betty.

The Hallmarks were first attracted to Excel by the extra income they could make. "Teachers are always looking for something to do to bring in some extra money," Betty told me. "Daryl was a high school teacher and coach. I taught kindergarten and first grade. We raised three kids to put through college. During the summers, Daryl was always painting houses and mowing lawns."

Both were intrigued by the ease and logic of the Excel business approach. "We thought it was kind of neat to get paid for other people making phone calls. Our original goal was to make about $400 extra a month. By the third month, we got a check from Excel that was more than Daryl's paycheck from teaching and coaching. That's when we checked our retirement and checked out of our jobs."

In the business for four years, the Hallmarks have attained the coveted Senior Director position, and in addition to establishing a more secure foundation for retirement, they have taken two trips to Australia with their children. Says Betty: "Excel opened our eyes to a whole new world. This business helped us take off the blinders. I can't believe it took so long!"

Controlling Your Paycheck

"I thought I would die behind a desk," says LaDonna Triplett, of Eldorado, Illinois. Like the Hallmarks, LaDonna was a public school teacher, logging 16 years in the profession and teaching everything from kindergarten up to junior college. "I loved teaching," she told me. "But one day I checked into my retirement plan and realized I had to keep on doing it for another 22 years before I could get a pension!"

LaDonna was introduced to Excel in December 1992, and she reports that her experience was "charmed from the beginning." During her first month in the business, she had the opportunity to meet Paul Orberson. During the second month, she hosted Steve Smith at a dinner in her home. The next month, she met Kenny Troutt. To really get her business going, she decided to take a leave of absence from teaching.

No sooner did she do that than her husband, Jamie, lost his job with no notice after 22 years with a coal industry company.

"That experience made us realize that if we ever wanted to really be in control of our finances, we had to be in control of our paychecks," LaDonna says. Today, LaDonna has grown her Excel business to the Executive Director level. Adding to her personal satisfaction and sense of achievement is that she is also a corporate trainer for the company. "It's great," she says, "because I still get to do what I do best, which is to teach. The difference is that now I am teaching people who want to be taught."

What lessons does this successful woman entrepreneur impart to her students? "The number one factor needed to succeed is an overwhelming desire to see the job through," LaDonna says. "I tell my students about the countless examples of successful Excel Reps who were really floundering after two years and were perhaps ready to quit but then in the third year found the right people and their businesses really took off!"

She adds, "Don't worry about building a vast empire. Worry about gathering customers. If you get good customers, you're bound to find some that want to be Representatives." In fact, for years LaDonna's mother was a loyal customer. Just recently, at age 83, she decided to become a Rep and build her own Excel business!

"It's never too late," LaDonna reminds us. "Just stay at it."

From Fame to Fortune

With a six-figure income, a popular television show, and a degree of celebrity, Don Dickson never figured himself a candidate for starting over. For 30 years he built a business around the outdoor life and sports fishing, marketing his ideas and love of the sport through lectures, instructional videos, and a TV program on station WGN in Chicago.

Call it an accident of timing, or chalk it up to the cruel vagaries of the television business, but in the early 1990s, things began to go south. "Life works in strange ways," Don told me. "Two days after I got word of a huge business loss, I found Excel. I decided to pursue it for one simple reason: to save the business I built all my life."

Twenty-six months later, Don not only had saved his business—he sold it! A more stable income with greater potential partially explains it. But what really makes the difference in Excel for Don is the people. "In this business, the real slick people don't last too long. Only the good people last."

Learning from the Young

When you devote your life to education and raising a family, you expect to be the ones to do all the teaching and mentoring. But Excel Senior Directors Bob Cross, a former high school principal, and his wife, Linda, a teacher, learned one of life's most important lessons from their son. A business major in college, Jason returned home one day and told his parents about an exciting new business opportunity he had just discovered: Excel.

"Jason encouraged us to listen to the Excel business presentation. He had just finished a unit on MLM [multilevel marketing]. His professors had taught him that multilevel marketing is one of the most effective ways to market a product," says Linda.

"We never marketed anything in our lives," Bob told me. "Here we were, living in Karnak, Illinois, with a total population of 581, a town that wasn't even serviced by Excel. Within 18 months, Linda and I were ready to devote our full-time energies to the business. We waited to go full-time until our checks were 11 times my monthly principal's check."

Linda says flatly, "If Bob and I, sitting in our small town with no business experience, can make it, anyone can."

Fortunate Misfortune

Ron and Judy Head thought the die was cast. "My path was pretty simple," says Ron. "I got out of high school, I went into the Marine Corps, and I never went to college. I got a job in sales and ended up making no more than $20,000 a year working six days a week."

Things might have stayed the same forever, until Ron lost his job. "There I was, 50 years old with nothing to do. I lost my pride. I lost my dignity. But worst of all, Judy had to go to work to help us make ends meet."

Desperate or not, when friends called the Heads to invite them to a meeting at the Executive Inn in Evansville, Illinois, to hear about the Excel business opportunity, their first reaction was clear. "We aren't going to any stupid meeting," Ron told them.

Ron ended up going anyway, and he was surprised by what he learned. "There was nothing to buy, nothing to sell, nothing to deliver. It was that simple. Kenny Troutt told me I'd never see an opportunity like this again, and he was right!"

Judy, who was even more skeptical than Ron at the outset, speaks even more passionately than he about what Excel has done for their lives: "For the last 41 months we've been in this business, I've been living the American dream," Judy says. "The best thing of all is that we're being paid to help and watch thousands of other people change their lives for the better, just as we have."

Always a Beginning

In his career, Ronny Kirkland, of Atlanta, Georgia, needed more than just a second chance. He needed a third, a fourth, and maybe a fifth chance, too!

"I've had at least three 10-year careers," he told me. He taught school, he sold mobile homes, and he took a shot at just about every sales scheme the telecommunications business had to offer before finding Excel three years ago.

"The low point of my life was in January 1989, when I went bankrupt," Ronny remembers. "I became committed to reselling phone service, but I kept failing—in AT&T, in MCI, in Sprint. I've finally come to understand why. With those companies, the bigger the sale, the better. The problem with that is there's no loyalty, and in such a competitive business, loyalty's going to count for everything.

"It's real simple. The smaller the phone bill is, the more the friendship matters. The larger the phone bill is, the more the rate matters. I finally found a way to be successful because Kenny Troutt found a way to put loyalty back into the telephone business."

It may be simple, but it wasn't easy. "I started on December 21, 1993, and I got rejected by 56 people in a row. Number 57 signed up. Before I knew it, I was bringing in $10,000 a month. But no amount of money can buy the feeling I got from succeeding in this business!"

Living Debt-Free

Ronny Kirkland not only found a new lease on life for himself through Excel but also created one for Senior Directors Hugh and Denise Hillis.

By the time they neared age 40, Hugh and Denise found themselves up to their eyeballs in consumer debt. "We owed $145,000," Hugh painfully recalls. "We were sinking so fast that my father-in-law had to take out a second mortgage on his house to help us pay our bills. You can't imagine what that did to our self-esteem."

With four sons to support and a 13-year career in insurance that seemed to be going nowhere, Hugh saw no way out of the cycle of work and debt. After their youngest son reached age 5, Denise went back into the workforce as well. Then during the Christmas season in 1993, an old friend named Ronny Kirkland called Hugh and exclaimed, "Forget Christmas, son. I just hit the mother lode. If we pull this one off, you won't be counting your money anymore, you'll be weighing it!"

Ronny then drove nine hours in a beat-up old car to the Hillises' rural Tennessee home just to show them the Excel plan. They swam toward the life preserver thrown at them just as fast as they could. "I knew within 90 days that this is what we needed and were looking for," Hugh says.

Within two years, the couple was debt-free. "I can't describe how good it felt the day I paid off my father-in-law's mortgage and handed him back the deed to his house," Hugh explains. "Excel allowed me that chance to get out of debt, and I never want to go there again."

That explains why, despite their business success, the Hillises live in the same home and drive the same car they did before Excel. "What's really important is that we've freed ourselves from the debt trap. I tell people who come to our meetings not to worry so much about homes and cars. There's something more important: your self-respect and your self-esteem."

Says Denise, "Excel has absolutely changed our lives. It's the freedom that comes from being so deep in debt and then climbing out of it. My desire is that others realize this freedom too."

Preparing for Poverty

Glen and Charlene Phibbs, from Tulsa, Oklahoma, worked hard and without complaint all their lives. "I spent 30 years in sales and marketing, including 10 years in real estate," Glen told me. "Charlene was a registered nurse working 12-hour shifts."

After a lifetime of toil, what did the Phibbs have to show for it? A loving family, including seven children and 15 grandchildren, to be sure. But as for financial security: "Nothing. We had put away very little for retirement," Glen says.

The couple joined Excel over two years ago, Charlene says, "because this business gave us our best opportunity to catch up. If like us others have been unable to prepare for retirement, you still have a chance to catch up through Excel." Six months after starting the business, Charlene was able to quit nursing and catch up even faster. The Phibbs are Executive Directors and are proud to have in their organization six of Excel's top money earners.

From Over the Hill to Top of the Mountain

Everyone tried to tell Barbara Witt that she was over the hill. It's a sad commentary on a society that at once purports to honor parenthood but at the same time exalts the culture of youth and often seeks to push the wisdom of age aside.

For 32 years, Barbara was a stay-at-home mom, raising four children and managing the family household. But at 52, with her children grown and her marriage breaking up, Barbara found herself on her own with no career. Despite all the doubters, she plunged headlong into a job selling new custom-built homes, and she soon became the company's top salesperson.

Deeply religious, Barbara turned to the Bible for guidance during the difficult time when her life was undergoing such change and uncertainty. "I realized it was time to get out of the boat and try to walk on water," she says. Resistant to network marketing at first, once she found the strength to "get out of the boat" she attacked the business with a vengeance. "I started two years ago when I was 62 years old, and from day one I was signing people up like crazy. I talk to people all the time. I just signed up a 64-year-old lady the other day.

"I tell them all the same thing: it's time to get out of the boat and walk on water."

Barbara also credits the business with bringing her family closer together than ever before. Last year, she took 17 members of her extended family to Disney World, putting them up in the best hotels. "I've never been down a day since I've been in this business," she marvels. No one is telling Barbara Witt she's over the hill any longer!

A Little Is Enough

One of the common reservations expressed by those considering joining a network marketing company is the belief that the chances of making serious money are negligible; therefore, the prospects of really changing one's life or building financial security for retirement years are not that bright, so why bother?

The reason is because even modest sums of additional income, if handled responsibly, can with patience and perseverance lead to a more secure and bountiful life. Let's assume, very conservatively, that you earn six percent on annual deposits of the entire year's proceeds from your Excel business. (The following exercise would apply regardless of the source of income.)

If you save just $900 yearly ($75 average monthly savings), you'd have:

o $5,073 after 5 years
o $15,109 after 10 years
o $20,948 after 15 years
o $33,107 after 20 years

If you save $1,800 yearly ($150 average monthly savings), you'd have:

o $10,147 after 5 years
o $30,218 after 10 years
o $41,897 after 15 years
o $66,214 after 20 years

If you save $6,000 yearly ($500 average monthly savings), you'd have:

o $33,823 after 5 years
o $100,726 after 10 years
o $139,656 after 15 years
o $220,714 after 20 years

If you save $12,000 yearly ($1,000 average monthly savings), you'd have:

o $67,645 after 5 years
o $201,452 after 10 years
o $279,312 after 15 years
o $441,427 after 20 years

Of course, should you save or invest your extra Excel income at a higher rate of return, your "paltry" monthly sums would grow that much more. For example, at 8 percent interest, your $6,000 in yearly savings would provide you with a nest egg of:

- ○ $35,200 after 5 years
- ○ $107,074 after 10 years
- ○ $162,913 after 15 years
- ○ $274,572 after 20 years

If you are able to sock away $12,000 a year at 8 percent, you'd have:

- ○ $70,399 after 5 years
- ○ $214,147 after 10 years
- ○ $325,825 after 15 years
- ○ $549,144 after 20 years

Want to become a millionaire on an Excel or other income of just $1,200 a month? Save it each month at 12 percent interest, and in 20 years, you will have accumulated $1,037,555!

The point is this: Even if you do not work your Excel business to the point where it becomes your principal occupation and your primary source of income, the extra income you do earn, saved responsibly and wisely, can still improve your life in significant ways.

For example, you could be 50 years old today, continue to work that full-time job, spend your entire salary, and sustain your current lifestyle. Meanwhile, with the help of your spouse and family, you could be starting an Excel business, perhaps generate (by way of illustration only) $1,000 extra dollars a month, and socking all of it away at 8 percent interest. By the time you're ready to retire at 65, you could have more than $300,000 on hand in addition to your pension and Social Security. What an extra margin of comfort and security that would provide!

Full Circle

Sarah Smith has been as close to the center of Excel as anyone. I'm talking not about the corporate center but about the vital center of the business: the power it has to change people's lives. After all, she is married to Steve Smith, the chief architect of the company's network marketing approach to business.

Some skeptics believe that a network marketing company consists of a highly manipulative group of successful pros at the center who concoct a skillfully crafted dream factory that grinds out a product for the masses without believing in it or feeling its power themselves. It's akin to the image we have of the entertainment industry, of sophisticated corporate barracudas releasing trashy movies, music, and television shows they would never listen to or watch.

Anyone who talks to Sarah Smith quickly realizes that the belief in the power of this business to change people's lives begins at the top. In very emotional terms, she underscores an important theme of this book: no matter what twists and turns your life has taken, it's not too late to have a new beginning.

To Sarah, life has been a series of detours, some good and some bad. For a time, her life was picture-postcard, middle-class perfect. After a comfortable upbringing in El Paso, Texas, Sarah graduated from Stephens College in 1973, began a career as a teacher, and in 1974 married Steve. "It was perfect," she recalls. "We had two children, two cars, and a colonial home with a white picket fence. I was a full-time homemaker, which is what I really wanted to do."

Then Steve came home one night and told Sarah about his falling out with his father. He was quitting the family business. Overnight, the security of Steve's six-figure paycheck had disappeared. "Over three years, our homes got smaller and smaller. We moved to Austin, and I went back to teaching."

Sarah recalls how low the family had sunk: "We lived in a friend's condo rent-free for 16 months. When we ran out of money, the electricity and the water were turned off. We had no phone either, so I had to go to the local convenience store to call in for substitute teaching jobs."

She was running out of patience, and she deeply resented that Steve threw overboard their comfortable life to pursue dreams she really didn't understand. "We basically lost everything and we almost lost our marriage."

Reflecting on that painful period now, Sarah realizes that she failed to see at first that "Steve is someone you can't put boundaries around. He had to follow his heart. That's the way it is with entrepreneurs. They want to try something new and be on their own."

When Steve crossed paths with network marketing and, later, Kenny Troutt, she knew he had found his calling. "You should have seen him in the early days of Excel," she recalls in wonder. He worked Monday through Friday in Dallas with Kenny and commuted back to Austin on weekends. Sometimes he'd tell me two hours in advance that we were going to have a barbecue in our home so he could network for the business. When he had back problems, I saw him presenting the Excel plan to prospects in a horizontal position. To this day, Steve still personally makes the pitch when he comes upon that one new potential customer!"

Sarah was happy for her husband: "Nothing dies slower or more painfully than your dream, and Steve just wouldn't let his die."

"This business has given us so many choices where we used to have none," she tells new Excel Reps and their families. "You too could be on the verge of the greatest years of your life. Just listen to your heart."

NO MORE EXCUSES

S TEVE SMITH HAS heard all the excuses. So, in his firm, fatherly manner, he looks out over the crowd of 1,500 at the Excel Opportunity Rally in Los Angeles and says, "You know, it seems like whenever people quit Excel they send me a letter. They say, 'Steve, I'm quitting today and I want to tell you whose fault it is.' The letter may complain that the individual's sponsor didn't train him or her properly, or the materials didn't arrive on time, or the plan didn't work the way it was supposed to.

"Believe me, I've heard them all. So if any of you are sitting there thinking you might quit and you're struggling to come up with a reason, come down here and see me when we adjourn, and I'll give you a new excuse to put in your letter! But I just wish that once someone who quit would be totally honest with me and send me a letter that says, 'Steve, I'm quitting today because that's what I do. I've done it before and I'll do it again!'"

If I've done my job in writing this book, you should be convinced of this much by now:

○ Telecommunications is one of the most dynamic industries in the United States and around the world today.
○ Network marketing is one of the fastest-growing business approaches in America.
○ Excel is a solid company on a fast but stable track, passing muster on both Main Street and Wall Street.

Even so, you may be thinking: It still doesn't sound right for me. I'm not sure I can do it. It sounds too good to be true.

You are not alone. Your questions are not uncommon. Many of Excel's most successful Representatives told me of their own intense skepticism when first introduced to the business—skepticism about the company and their own ability to succeed in it.

Philip Eckart, of Austin, Texas, was one of them. He got into the Excel business seven years ago. "At that time, it was very difficult to be successful in Excel. I quit after eight months and started working another network marketing business where it appeared the grass was greener. It wasn't. Two-and-a-half years later, I looked at the Excel opportunity again and saw a company that had evolved to where the opportunity was more easily achievable. So I got back in." Today, Philip and his wife, Heidi, work their Excel business full-time and have reached the coveted position of Senior Director.

Asking the Tough Questions

If you are considering a decision that could fundamentally change your life, you should ask the tough questions. I'd like to try to answer a few of them here.

Are network marketing businesses real or are they phony pyramid schemes set up to rip off people like me?

When I began my examination of this unorthodox approach to business, many of my own friends and associates—most of them from highly skilled professions—were quick to condemn multilevel marketing companies as phony or even illegal pyramid schemes. Finally, I challenged the remark.

"You just called this company a pyramid," I said. "Just what is that, anyway?"

"It's when, um, well, you see . . ." My friend struggled and stammered for a minute to try to explain what a so-called pyramid scheme was, but he couldn't do it.

161

Clearly both the news media and word of mouth had poisoned his attitude against these companies, from Amway to Mary Kay to Excel. He had heard that these companies were pyramids and that pyramids were bad; therefore, the companies must be bad. Case closed.

Unfair as the situation may be, there is no question that this approach to business suffers from a serious image problem in many quarters. Someday, hopefully, the image will catch up to the facts, which are these:

- Network marketing is catching on like wildfire across America and around the world.
- It is being embraced by both companies and people who have never considered it before.
- It is changing the way we buy and sell goods and services.
- It is giving hope and opportunity to millions of people who otherwise may have none.

What constitutes an illegal pyramid? While the law is subject to differing interpretations, a pyramid scheme is generally seen as a business that is built almost exclusively on paying people to sign up distributors—with little or no focus on gathering actual customers to buy products and services. New recruits are required to buy major quantities of a product up front, with no opportunity to return unsold inventory for a refund. Intense pressure is applied to get them to buy expensive tapes, instruction manuals, and tickets to meetings and rallies. Essentially, participants feed off each other, with the big fish consuming the resources and energies of the smaller fish.

The entire multilevel marketing industry faced a day of legal reckoning in 1979, when the Federal Trade Commission ruled that Amway was a legitimate business and not a pyramid. On all counts, Excel passes the test too. While great emphasis is placed on bringing new Representatives into the business and developing them through training to their fullest potential, the end consumer always remains the core of the business. All one has to do is visit Excel's call and customer service centers in Dallas, Houston, or Reno to understand how important customer service and satisfaction are to the company. After all, with the demand for an ever-expanding array of telecommunications services on a never-ending spiral upward—not to mention the *intense* competition within this industry—ignoring the customer would be just plain stupid.

Nevertheless, the stigma remains. Part of the reason is because network marketing still seems like a new and untested approach. Those companies who have sunk fortunes into hiring sales forces, buying ads on network television, and developing intricate retail distribution networks have a vested interest in keeping the doubts alive, even though many of them are migrating toward direct selling approaches themselves.

In *Wave 3: The New Era in Network Marketing* (Prima), Richard Poe draws an interesting parallel in his discussion of network marketing's rocky road to legitimacy:

> New ideas are always attacked and rejected at first. In its earliest days, franchising endured similar abuse from the press and from the corporate world, and for almost identical reasons. . . .
>
> The media attacked like hungry barracuda. Exposés featured destitute families who'd lost their life savings through franchising schemes. Attorneys general in state after state condemned the new marketing method. Some congressmen actually tried to outlaw franchising entirely.
>
> How quickly things change! Today, franchises account for 35 percent of all retail sales in the United States.

Even if the industry is legitimate, how do I know Excel itself is for real?

This concern touches upon another reason for lingering doubts about the network marketing approach to business: there are some bad apples. Out there are companies built on flimsy premises with lousy products, impossible marketing plans, and dubious ethics.

How can you tell if Excel or any other company you're considering is solid and substantial? Here's a five-step checklist:

1. Check with the Direct Selling Association (DSA) in Washington, D.C., at (202) 293-5760.

This is a trade group that not only promotes this industry but polices it and spurs the process of developing, applying, and enforcing industry "best practices." Ask the DSA whether the company you want to join is a member. Why is that important? Because in order to become a DSA member, the company must sign and adhere to a strict code of ethics. Excel is a leading DSA member and a signatory to the code of ethics.

2. Look at the company's track record.

Is it on a steady growth path? Does it have professional management that is accessible and open to independent representatives, customers, and the business press? Does it present itself well and professionally in the community, the media, the meetings, and conventions it holds through its corporate offices and other business facilities and through communications organs, such as magazines, product presentations, and videos?

Kenny Troutt took a bold and somewhat unusual step by taking Excel public in 1996. Beyond the strategic business reasons, doing so has in the eyes of many observers bestowed great credibility on the company. Going public means that detailed financial information is regularly filed with the Securities and Exchange Commission and is therefore publicly accessible. Most network companies remain in private hands. Nothing bad should be implied in the decision of those remaining private, but Excel's decision to go public speaks volumes about this company's openness to scrutiny.

3. Examine the marketing plan.

Does the plan make sense to you? Is it simple and user-friendly? Can you anticipate receiving the support and training you need (at a reasonable cost) to succeed? Network marketers have a saying: You may be in business *for* yourself, but you are not in business *by* yourself. Make sure that will be the case in the company you join.

4. Consider the product(s).

Is demand for them going to grow, or are they part of a passing consumer fad? Are they products you would want your own family to use? One important trend to consider was summarized recently by University of Illinois Professor Charles W. King in *Success* magazine: "Network marketing is going through a revolutionary change. Companies are cutting loose from their narrow focus on a few specialized products to compete in the larger world of services."

Professor King points out that during the 1970s and 1980s most new network marketing firms continued to be product-driven, selling from the traditional categories of personal care, nutritional supplements, home and family care, and leisure and educational products. Amway had historically offered a range of services, but its major sales volume continued to be product-based.

Change began rapidly as the eighties turned into the nineties. Companies such as Excel, MCI, and Sprint have defined the post-regulation telecommunications industry through network marketing; as well, other companies have been developing such approaches for services such as travel, legal counseling, and insurance. Electrical service is on the near horizon. "We can anticipate that services will widen the beachhead of network marketing companies in the years ahead, allowing them to gain a vastly greater share of our economy," concludes Professor King.

When it comes to Excel's mainstay product (long-distance phone service), many of the company's most successful Representatives view its advantage simply and clearly. The ultimate advantage of selling this product is that it's reordered every time a customer picks up the phone!

5. Talk to the people who are working the business.

You're likely to find people just like you, people from your station in life, people with whom you share strengths, weaknesses, hopes, and fears. Find out how they made it work or failed to make it work and why. Here's one Excel example:

Methodical is the best way to describe Jimmy Dick's journey to Excel. It took him 20 years of study and scrutiny before he found a business that "met all the criteria." A former stockbroker and teacher who ran a financial services company, Jimmy told me, "I have always been fascinated by network marketing." In fact, his fascination led him to examine 121 different network marketing companies. "Some were really good. Some were scams. You really have to be careful. Excel was different. It met all the criteria for me."

Why did Excel stand out? "Loyal customers—that's the key," Jimmy says. "You derive your customers from people who love you: your family, your friends, your relatives. No other business does that. I got my family to be my loyal customers. If you can do that too, you'll be successful. You sign up a few people and you train them. Then they sign up a few people. It's the simplicity of the concept that makes Excel work."

I never see Excel ads on TV. It buys service from the really big companies and resells it. Excel may be a decent network marketing company, but is it a real phone company?

The American economy's dramatic transition from a manufacturing-based economy to a service-oriented one is forcing us all to change our mind-set about what constitutes a real company with real products. Automation and information technologies have altered traditional definitions further still.

We used to judge a company's muscle in the marketplace based on how many plants, warehouses, employees, subsidiaries, and retail outlets it maintained. Today, a premium is placed on shedding those things. Many businesses are outsourcing functions they used to perform in-house. What you own or what you make is less important than what you organize and orchestrate on behalf of the customer. It's all about logistics.

Suppose you run a publishing company that needs to move a load of books from Boston to Washington, D.C. in three days. You've long since discarded your own privately owned trucking fleet. It was just too expensive and required you to be expert in a business totally different from publishing. Calling a dozen trucking companies, a couple of air freight outfits, and maybe a railroad is a waste of your time and money too. Instead, you contact a transportation logistics company, tell them the kind of service you need, cross-checked by what you're prepared to pay, and you let the company figure it out. You don't particularly care whether the company owns its own trucks, leases them, decides to outsource the business to a partner company, and you don't care whether they put your books on an airplane or on the rails. What you care about and what you're paying for is a safe, dependable, on-time service at a competitive price.

The transportation provider that performed your task for you is no less a real company because it used someone else's trucks or because it asked an owner-operator it had under contract to carry your freight. In today's competitive, just-in-time economy, it's a more useful, efficient, and customer-oriented company because it put you first.

Consider another service industry: banking. The bank that grants you a loan does not own that money. It "buys" the money from its depositors and "resells" it to you, the borrower. In fact, telephone reselling is a common practice and a well-established industry with its own national trade group, the Telecommunications Resellers Association. A recent report from the Dow Jones news service explains:

> Because all the U.S.'s phone cable is owned by just a handful of companies, most phone companies— more than 800—sell their service by buying time on others' cable networks. . . . These firms buy the minutes in bulk at wholesale prices and sell them at higher rates. They also have reduced costs because they don't maintain facilities, although they normally handle billing, customer service and sales.

Bundling and selling excess capacity to those who find a way to resell it at a profit is a mutually beneficial transaction for the original supplier and the reseller alike. Unsold capacity is much like the empty airline seat that becomes a squandered asset once the plane takes off.

Excel's supremacy in this endeavor as well as the stability of its supply of long-distance capacity is illustrated by the caliber of its business partners, companies such as Worldcom, MCI, Frontier, and IXC Communications. Nonetheless, if the credo "change or die" rings true in business generally, that goes double for the fast-paced, competitive world of telecommunications. It explains Kenny Troutt's ceaseless drive to improve the marketing plan and diversify the product offerings, even beyond telecommunications. And it explains Excel's recent plan to purchase nine switches from Lucent Technologies and to acquire Telco Communications Group, a company with its own fiber-optic network already in the ground.

Serving as a major long distance reseller will surely remain a core component of Excel's business. Yet the new switches and the Telco acquisition are seen as necessary prerequisites to entering emerging markets such as local phone service and digital mobile phone technology, known as the personal communications system (PCS).

Finally, keep in mind that almost anyone who sells anything retail is selling something that has already been made and sold at least once before. If you want to suggest that reselling phone service is anything less than a real, legitimate business, you'd have to say the same thing about any 7-Eleven, Macy's, or Wal-Mart.

I heard that Excel got into trouble with the Better Business Bureau. What's the story?

All of the companies in the highly competitive long-distance telephone market have been grappling with an illegal practice known as "slamming," which refers to switching a person's long-distance service without his or her knowledge or consent. A significant increase in consumer complaints about slamming led the Federal Communications Commission to crack down on the practice.

In September 1996, the chapter of the Better Business Bureau serving the Dallas area briefly revoked Excel's membership in the Bureau because of what it said was an increase in the number of customer complaints, a number of them related to slamming. The action precipitated a temporary drop in the company's stock price. That membership was reinstated just three months later, once Excel had an opportunity to review for Bureau officials the entirety of its record and the intensity of its commitment to prevent slamming within the ranks of its Independent Representatives.

The company's policy, which it underscores repeatedly to anyone selling Excel products and services, reads like law and order, Texas-style:

> The slamming of a customer to Excel long-distance service is prohibited by Excel's Policies and Procedures as set forth in every Excel Independent Representative's application and agreement, and will result in the immediate termination of representative status and forfeiture of all commissions. Excel will refer Reps who slam customers for criminal prosecution.

I don't like the idea of selling things. I didn't receive all this education just to end up as a sales rep.

Although it enjoys a proud tradition in many cultures, selling is inexplicably frowned upon by many in our status-oriented society. This attitude is often seen in people who have impressive-sounding jobs but modest incomes and no control over their time. Since I work in and around many highly skilled and status-oriented professionals in law, politics, and the corporate world, I run into condescending attitudes all the time.

For many from the so-called boomer and yuppie generations, building an independent business through network marketing simply doesn't jive with their carefully cultivated image as worldly-wise, white-collar professionals. They crave title, rank, status, and, most important, security. They seek the identity and social approval that comes from their association with a prestigious blue-chip company, a big-name law firm, or an important government agency. It's as if their worst nightmare is to be asked by a total stranger on an airplane what they do or where they work and have the person say, "I've never heard of it."

This attitude is changing. As the security of the status jobs dissipates and the frenetic, pressure-cooker lifestyles they bring lose their appeal, many professional people who used to dismiss network marketing are taking another look at companies like Excel. There's only so many times one can see others build much happier, more rewarding lives before one stops and says, "Hey, why can't I do something like that?"

When we look at the most successful people in Excel, we see doctors, lawyers, professors, and corporate executives as well as coaches, homemakers, real estate salespeople, and small business owners. We see the young and the old, the married and the single, the college-educated and the high school dropout, the African-American, Hispanic, Asian, as well as white American. We see those coming to the business at a time when they were down and out and those who were sitting at the top of another field but wanted to succeed in something different. In short, if you're looking for someone just like you who has succeeded in Excel, you'll find that person!

Excel is uniquely positioned to tap into the rich vein of disgruntled professionals. Look at the products: not diet supplements, household goods, or cosmetics, but state-of-the-art telecommunications services. What could be more cutting edge than that?

So picture the next time you're sitting on that plane (probably in first class). You're reading a good book while the person next to you is filling out corporate expense reports. He asks you what you do, and you say: "Me? I own my own telecommunications business." Then sign him up!

I won't be very good at selling. Can I do it?

Fear of rejection—it's the most natural of human hangups. I know it well. I've enjoyed great prestige and power serving in top government political and policy positions. Several years ago, after an eight-year stint in the California governor's office, I attempted a transition. I left my powerful position to build a public relations consultancy in which I had to sell my professional services. After years of having the high and mighty knock on my door, suddenly I had to knock on theirs—without title, without status, without influence. I had to rely on people I thought were my loyal friends. At least they acted that way when I was in my political office. But I quickly learned the bitter truth of President Harry S. Truman's memorable advice: "If you want a friend in politics, get a dog!"

Within a year, I dumped my consultancy and beat a hasty retreat back to appointed political office, at less pay and stature than I had before. I was going backward. It was only after reflecting on this experience and meeting many people in network marketing that I realized what held me back was not the perceived slights of so-called friends but my own fear of rejection. I did everything possible to avoid having to promote myself or my services because I was afraid of being turned down. Virtually everyone on Excel's Eagle Team of top performers could relate to you countless rejections as they have built their businesses. "Just keep on going and keep on pushing" is their universal advice.

One great advantage Excel has for those struggling with insecurity about selling is that those you first target as customers and customer gatherers are those who are the least likely to reject you. If you know a few family members and good friends who you're comfortable approaching and who might be willing to help you out, you're on your way! Your discomfort level is further addressed by the frequent meetings, training sessions, rallies, and other forums Excel organizes around the country. Invite your friends and associates to these meetings and let others present the business plan for you.

Are you thinking that you don't know enough people to build a large enough network marketing business? You might be surprised how many assets you can bring to the table. It has been estimated that the typical American adult over the age of 25 knows about 2,000 people by their first names. Chances are you've already got a potential network of Excel customer gatherers and you don't even know it.

Does anyone really get rich in this kind of business besides a few at the top?

Turnover is high throughout the network marketing industry. People move in and out of the business all the time. In some cases it's because they've achieved the relatively modest set of goals they established at the outset: to earn some extra money to pay off a few bills, buy a new car, or finance a dream vacation. Others join because they like people and want opportunities to socialize and broaden their network of friends, but they never focus on making the business their full-time occupation. Some are initially attracted by the low entry fee but don't enter the business with any serious level of commitment. Then there are those who leave Excel or other businesses of its type who have soured on the experience and believe that the deck was stacked against them. The riches they had envisioned didn't materialize, and they blame the company.

Excel tries to make your entry into the business world as easy and painless as possible, and it tries to see that you get paid for your efforts as quickly as possible. It is not a get-rich-quick scheme, however, and it has never claimed to be.

It is true that most people who join network marketing companies do not develop incomes to the level at which they can leave their regular jobs behind and thus dramatically change their lives. Like most other endeavors in life, you get out of it what you put into it. In fact, the Direct Selling Association has reported that while those who go at these businesses full-time are a distinct minority, more than half of the full-timers make over $50,000 a year. One in ten makes over $100,000.

Think about those odds. Reflect on the fact that the average full-time salary in the United States is still just $28,000 per year. With the exception of professions requiring extremely high skill levels, your chances of making serious money working full-time in network marketing would easily match and beat most occupations in America today. Is it possible for you to achieve the milestones attained by the Excel leaders profiled in this book? Absolutely. Are there any guarantees? Absolutely not. Is it worth it for you to give it a try? In the final analysis, only you can answer that question. Much depends on the status of your own life and your own unique definition of what constitutes success and personal happiness.

Remember, not all the value of this business can be calculated in dollars and cents. A great deal of personal growth comes with building an Excel business. How do you measure in dollars and cents the value of these potential benefits:

- ○ You as parents can have more time to spend with your children.
- ○ You don't have to say, "No, we can't afford it" when your child asks for new clothes.
- ○ After a lifetime of working for someone else, you get the chance to build something for yourself and your family on your own, even if you're pulling in less income.
- ○ You can face the prospect of old age with financial security, so you needn't fear becoming a burden on your children.
- ○ You can make lifelong friends among highly successful people, people from all walks of life all over the country, whom you would never have met otherwise.
- ○ You can enjoy the wonderful satisfaction that comes from helping others achieve their dreams too.

How do you measure any of that in dollars and cents?

I have often reflected on the fact that when I was a college student I earned a couple hundred dollars a month bussing tables in the campus dining hall to help pay for books and tuition. In retrospect, I would have been much better prepared for adult life ahead if I had begun a low-cost network marketing business instead. Even if I didn't earn a penny more, I would have been learning the fundamentals of operating my own business, and those skills would have been far more valuable than wiping tables.

Let's say you're half of a working couple and both you and your spouse are holding down 40-hour-a-week jobs outside the home. You're pulling in $30,000 a year but paying thousands a year for child care you don't really trust. How much income from building a business like Excel would it take to convince you to quit that job and stay home with your kids, considering the money you wouldn't spend on child care and all the other ancillary benefits you would enjoy by being a full-time parent and an independent business owner? For most, it would take considerably less than that $30,000—and there would be the far superior potential of earning much more. Each one of us has to cross-check our individual circumstances and priorities against the chances of success in Excel and make a personal evaluation as to its worth.

Isn't the market already saturated? Don't you have to get into this kind of company right at the start to really succeed?

Excel today claims about 3 percent of the long-distance market. On the strength of just that 3 percent, a $1.4 billion company has been built and tens of thousands of individuals and families have founded their own businesses, some achieving financial independence and becoming millionaires in the process. Just imagine what 4, 5, 6, 16, or 20 percent of the market could sustain.

Still, the concern is a real one for many prospective Excel Independent Representatives. Current IRs tell me they hear that question all the time. During a recent speech to Reps and their guests in Los Angeles, Kenny Troutt declared that the opportunities in Excel are just as great for those starting in the business today as they were for top earners like Paul Orberson several years ago. One gentlemen disagreed and blurted out, "Oh yeah, right!"

Without missing a beat, Kenny spelled out his vision of the company's future opportunities. There's going to be far more to Excel than the long-distance market, he explained. There's a whole range of additional products being offered, from paging to international calling. Then there's all the exciting new directions just on the horizon, including local calling, international markets, and residential electricity. "And there are other products we don't even know about yet," Kenny concluded. I don't know if he changed the dissenter's mind, but judging from the reaction of the audience, he convinced everyone else.

Will I be pressured into spending a lot of money on training materials, meetings, and rallies?

Excel is one of the cheapest ways to get into business for yourself. There are no products to buy, no inventory to stock, and no significant financial investments to make. Getting started as an Independent Representative requires just a $50 refundable application deposit. Optional but strongly recommended, however, is an accompanying training and home business management package, which qualifies you as a Managing Representative and costs $195 with a $180 annual renewal fee. Among other important tools, this package includes the monthly *Communicator* magazine, which contains new product announcements and important business-building ideas.

Representatives are encouraged to take advantage of other education, training, and motivational opportunities, such as the Excel's Winners Weekends held around the country, the annual Excelebration in Dallas, and video programming produced by the company's Excelevision television network. There are fees for these activities, but all are voluntary. Still, many Reps find them invaluable, not only for improving their own skills but to introduce friends and associates to the business as well.

It's curious that some critics of companies like Excel would focus on the training and motivational tools to suggest some sort of undue pressure or wasteful expense is involved. How many of us have gone deeply into debt and spent untold thousands of dollars to pursue higher education for ourselves and our children? Is it unreasonable to spend several hundred dollars per year to go into business for oneself and secure the necessary training and information to succeed? You be the judge.

I'm too busy. Will I have the time for Excel?

Ah yes, the old "I don't have time" excuse! It's probably the most common brush-off prospecting network marketers hear. Recall our discussion in chapter 6 of the time poverty experienced by many two-income families struggling with both demanding careers and raising children. There's no question that's a huge burden. However, a new book by time study experts John Robinson and Geoffrey Godbey suggests that most of us probably could find the time to undertake a new activity like starting an Excel business. It's a question of priorities. These researchers examined the lifestyles of some 10,000 survey participants and concluded that Americans actually have more free time now than at any time in the last 30 years—an average of 40 hours a week.

If you find that hard to believe, consider that one of the study's most important conclusions is that people's perception of how busy they are often differs from reality. Study participants were asked to keep detailed diaries of their activities. When the results were analyzed, it was found that on average, working men perceived that they spend 46.2 hours on their paid, professional work. In actuality they spent 40.2 hours. Women perceived 40.4 hours but actually worked just 32 hours.

What's the reason for the exaggeration? "Being busy has become a status symbol," Robinson told *Newsweek* recently. "As you say time is more important to you, you become more important yourself."

"In fact," the magazine goes on to report, "Americans are working fewer hours than they did in 1965: about five fewer hours per week for working women, six fewer for men."

Here's one other key finding: on average, working Americans spend 15 of their 40 free hours a week watching television! If, like me, you're one of them, perhaps we should reexamine our priorities and how readily we offer that most common of excuses: "I don't have time."

It's also important to remember the simplicity of Excel compared to other network marketing opportunities. There are no products to stock or time-consuming deliveries to make. Your customers reorder every time they pick up the phone. So if time is a factor, then being in a service-oriented business rather than a product-based business can minimize the time it takes to give it a serious effort.

Overcoming the Negativity

As you consider these important issues and determine whether this business opportunity is right for you, try to rise above the negativity that has invaded so much of our lives. The only way you can credibly doubt whether this company and the people in it face a positive future is to believe one or more of the following statements:

- ○ Negative Statement #1: Telecommunications is a dead-end, shrinking market in the U.S. and around the world.
- ○ Negative Statement #2: Network marketing has peaked as a business force, and professionals are going to be rehired in droves by corporate America in secure, high-paying positions.
- ○ Negative Statement #3: The leadership of Excel is shortsighted, complacent, and content to rest on yesterday's achievements.
- ○ Negative Statement #4: Americans have stopped dreaming of a better life and have stopped trying to do anything about it.

If you really believe any of these statements, then yes, you can find reason to call into question the future of Excel and your potential role in it. But if you believe that global telecommunications will continue to be marked by unparalleled growth; if you believe in the power of the network marketing approach to bring millions of additional people into low-cost business ownership; if you believe in the vision of Kenny Troutt, Steve Smith, Jack McLaine, and the Excel leadership to continually try exciting new directions; and if you believe in the dreams of average Americans to achieve financial independence and that you can achieve that dream and help others do the same, then there are no more questions and no more excuses.

IMAGINE!

FRIDAY, MAY 16, 9:30 P.M. Inside the auditorium of the L.A. Convention Center, the beat goes on. Excel Presidential Director Al Thomas wraps up his talk. "I'll see you at the top—or I'll see you *from* the top." The crowd of 1,500, more energized than at the start, roars its approval. Forty rows back, a young man whispers a Spanish translation into the ear of his elderly mother. She smiles and nods in agreement. Steve Smith takes the stage to an outpouring of reverence and affection. In a strong, reassuring tone, he makes a claim that captures the imagination of the crowd: "You're not going to recognize this company a few months from now."

The people cheer, and I wonder. In an era when so many are afraid of change and attempting to fend it off, the leaders of Excel have embraced change and have made it their loyal customer.

As Steve finishes and the hour grows late, a buzz of excitement works its way around the hall. "It's almost time for Kenny," a man impeccably dressed in a three-piece suit tells his wife.

During a coffee break earlier in the evening, Steve Smith and Kenny Troutt decide to make the rounds of the lobby. Standing at separate ends of the room, each is quickly immobilized by a throng of Excel Representatives and prospects surrounding them. The crowd surrounding Steve engages him in earnest conversation, to relate a specific experience out in the field and perhaps pick up one more piece of important advice from the master network marketer. The crowd around Kenny has another mission: autographs and pictures. Steve Smith may be their teacher. Kenny Troutt is their leader.

It could go on for hours. Finally, Kenny is led to the stage and is introduced to a standing ovation. "We built it together," Kenny Troutt tells the cheering crowd. "That's the strength of this company. It's what makes us different." He reviews with great satisfaction the pace of achievement in just nine years, citing these facts:

○ Excel is one of the youngest companies ever to be listed on the New York Stock Exchange.

○ It recorded $1.4 billion in sales in 1996 and
is only the third company to achieve such a
height through internal growth in so short
a time.

○ It shows a 200 percent increase in revenue
from communications services in just one
year.

○ Excel customers used 6.3 billion minutes of
long distance time, a 198 percent increase in
just one year.

○ Excel is the fifth-largest long distance company
in America in terms of presubscribed lines.

○ In just a matter of months, the company has
introduced powerful new products, such as
paging, international calling, and a flat,
10-cents-per-minute rate for long-distance
calls anytime, anyplace.

○ Enriching improvements have been made in
the marketing plan, giving Excel Representatives
more ways to make money faster.

"We've changed the way business is done in the communications industry," Kenny concludes. But his focus
has already shifted to the future. "I feel more excited
today than I did four years ago, when our company
really started to blast off. In the next five years, we're
going to experience a boom that's going to make the oil
boom of the past look like a poverty zone!"

Saying No to "No"

What makes Kenny Troutt so confident about the future? It begins with an attitude, one that looks forward, embraces change, and refuses to accept the limitations imposed by conventional wisdom.

One of my favorite stories is about a foreigner traveling in India who came upon a cafe in Bombay. This cafe makes its attitude towards its customers—and life—perfectly clear. Upon entering, diners are greeted by a large sign 20 lines long:

SORRY
NO Talking to Cashier
NO Smoking
NO Fighting
NO Credit
NO Outside Food
NO Sitting Long
NO Talking Loud
NO Spitting
NO Bargaining
NO Water to Outsiders
NO Change
NO Telephone
NO Match Sticks
NO Discussing Gambling
NO Newspaper
NO Combing

NO Beef
NO Leg on Chair
NO Hard Liquor Allowed
NO Address Inquiry

As Kenny Troutt gazes out over the booming Dallas metroplex from the top of Excel headquarters, the youthful 49-year-old executive sees a world of opportunity. Words like "no," "don't," and "can't" are alien to his vocabulary.

"Our greatest challenge is to put new products into the mix," he says. The strategy is to use Excel's powerful, built-in distribution system of Independent Representatives and their customers to move quickly into the most promising new arenas of products and markets. I'll discuss several of them in the sections to follow.

Paging

In the fall of 1996, Excel took an important initial step toward diversifying beyond residential long-distance services by launching ExcelPaging. More than 40 million Americans use this simple and affordable technology, up from 27 million since 1994. Industry analysts believe that by the year 2000 as many as 72 million people will carry pagers.

Paging is a logical extension for Excel. Pagers are small, portable, easy-to-use, and cost-effective. They're indispensable to many different types of businesses and professions. More and more, families are employing paging to stay in touch. The new generation of high-quality Motorola numeric and alphanumeric pagers, paging with voice mail, and nationwide single-frequency paging services add value to the basic paging function.

True to form, Excel was able to offer this new service without incurring the enormous capital expense of acquiring or developing paging transmission frequencies or infrastructure. The company believes that new products and services like paging will strengthen ties to existing customers and give potential new customers one more reason to switch.

Most important, the move to paging is a kind of warm-up pitch for even bolder moves into bigger markets. "Our initial foray outside Excel's fundamental line of long-distance services provides a model for developing, acquiring, and introducing other communications and services," company executives have stated.

Wireless Phones and the Personal Communications System (PCS)

Less than a decade ago, there were just 2.1 million cellular phone subscribers. "They were viewed mainly as toys for the rich or tools for executives and drug dealers," observed *Time* magazine recently.

Not anymore. Today, an estimated 43 million Americans use wireless phones, which means the wireless phone market has grown faster than the market for video recorders or fax machines at a comparable stage of development. Even so, the $25 billion cell phone market has still penetrated just 20 percent of the nation's homes. There's plenty of room for growth, as evidenced by the fact that companies are frenetically signing up new subscribers at the rate of 30,000 a *day.*

The tribulations of modern American life explain part of this technology's appeal to average citizens. Busy schedules and longer commutes make cell phones an attractive way to stay in touch and increase productivity. Many families view such phones as offering an extra measure of security should a loved one run into trouble away from home or encounter car problems on the road. Steady cuts in service cost, thanks to deregulation and the resulting intense competition, have put wireless calling well within reach of many family budgets.

Improved quality with an exciting array of new wireless services is on the horizon too, thanks to the creation of a new digital service called PCS (personal communications system), made possible by the Federal Communications Commission (FCC). The *Time* article explains: "The agency took a piece of the airwaves in the mid-frequency spectrum that had been used for police calls and other public purposes and turned it over to industry for cell-phone service."

The move—which netted the government more than $20 billion when it auctioned the licenses—will create a 15-fold increase in wireless capacity in the next several years. But that's not all. "Unlike many older systems, which send a voice in a single stream as analog waves, PCS uses digital signal," the *Time* article continues. "Digital technology enables PCS to offer such features as e-mail, caller ID and paging, as well as compact-disc-quality sound and greater security from wireless eavesdroppers and phone number thieves."

The expansion of new companies and technologies into the cell phone market has, however, carried with it the price of confusion. Echoing past advertising shootouts by major companies over long-distance service, wireless providers in many markets have thrown up a complex barrage of claims and counterclaims over competing pricing and service plans. A down-and-dirty price and image war is anticipated. With its emphasis on relationship selling and customer loyalty, Excel once again appears uniquely positioned to help its customers cut through the noise.

Local Phone Service

On February 8, 1996, President Bill Clinton signed the Telecommunications Act of 1996 into law.

This first major overhaul of telecommunications law in almost 62 years passed the U.S. House of Representatives by a vote of 414 to 16. The Senate passed the legislation by a 91 to 5 margin. At the signing ceremony, Vice President Al Gore said that "the Berlin Walls of the telecommunications industry have crumbled." In the eyes of FCC chairman Reed Hundt and others, the old law assumed that communications was a natural monopoly; the new law assumes that all parts of the communications marketplace can be made competitive.

The stated intent of the Act is to let anyone enter the communications business. Before the new law, it would have been illegal for some local phone companies to provide long-distance service outside their regions. Competition in the local phone markets was illegal in some states.

Today, both are legal. Local phone companies can offer out-of-region long-distance service; long distance companies like Excel can offer local telephone service. And these markets are not just limited to telephone companies. If the legislation works as planned, consumers in the future might receive local phone service from their Internet provider or what is now their cable company. They could get television programming from their local phone company and local phone service from their long distance carrier—or all these services from a single company, perhaps their local utility.

In fact, according to FCC commissioner Susan Ness, many cable companies, faced with new telephone company rivals for their video business, are poised to enter the local phone business. Their wires, with broadband capacity, already pass through more than 90 percent of the nation's homes. However, the cost of upgrading these wires for telephony by adding a power source and switching capability would require a heavy investment.

The prospect of these heavy investments in ever-changing technologies—along with the increasing market demand that a company bundle diverse services and offer customers one-stop shopping—has led some to forecast that the Telecommunications Act of 1996 would spur a wave of mergers throughout the industry. To the dismay of many observers who see such consolidation as a throwback to the past, those forecasters may be right.

In May 1997, for example, it was revealed that AT&T, still the dominant force in long distance, was engaged in merger talks with SBC Communications, the parent company of the two Baby Bells that dominate the local phone market in the southwestern United States, including Texas and California. The reports unleashed a firestorm of criticism and the two companies have since backed down.

The reason was anticipated by the *Los Angeles Times:* "Although the Telecommunications Act of 1996 cleared the way for new alliances in the long distance and local phone markets, severe regulatory hurdles could prevent an AT&T-SBC combination for several years, perhaps forever."

Industry analysts, legal experts, and consumer advocates immediately began assessing the proposed merger's impact, viability, and symbolism. Some see the attempt at a deal as further evidence of AT&T's weakening position. "The revelation that AT&T is considering a merger of equals with one of its progeny is seen as a sign that the once-invincible company has failed to capitalize on the opportunities of the new telecommunications market," the *Los Angeles Times* continued. *Los Angeles Times* business columnist James Flanigan complained that "maybe AT&T and SBC Communications were inspired by a dinosaur movie. In their merger talks they're trying to restore a lost world of monopoly suppliers of telecommunications services."

Flanigan continues:

> The Telecommunications Act of 1996 opened local phone service to all competitors. And one of the biggest new competitors was supposed to be AT&T, going after the lucrative local business. AT&T has mounted campaigns promising billions of dollars of investment to gain local customers. . . . Yet the talks disclosed . . . say that AT&T once again has chosen to acquire its way into local markets, purchasing SBC and eliminating a competitive contest for customers.

University of Southern California communications professor A. Michael Noll echoes Flanigan's sentiments: "Management of the communications industry seems unable to offer anything more creative than acquisitions as a way to shape the future." Stanford University professor William Baxter, who headed the Justice Department's effort to break up AT&T in 1984, said flatly, "This is Ma Bell all over again."

Consumers Union codirector Gene Kimmelman slammed the merger talks as well. "This basically moves in the opposite direction of the competition goals that Congress had in mind under the new Telecommunications Act," he said.

While many see the trend toward mergers of this kind as eliminating consumer choice and making it harder for companies like Excel to compete, other analysts disagree. "No matter what AT&T and SBC do, we've still got MCI, Sprint, GTE, and a huge number of new entrants," observed industry analyst Sandra Cook of the San Francisco Consulting Group. "Even if those two giants merge, there is still going to be plenty of competition in the marketplace."

Competition is just what Kenny Troutt has in mind. Giant companies trying to merge will spend years in federal and state justice department conference rooms and millions of dollars on legal fees, public relations campaigns, and public hearings, all so they can combine current markets instead of unearth new ones. Meanwhile, Kenny Troutt plans to move his nimble, proactive company swiftly into the local phone service sweepstakes—a more than $117 billion market.

"We could be announcing something by the end of this year," he told Excel Representatives in May 1997. "It's the most powerful product on the horizon. We could virtually double our business overnight." The acquisition of Telco, with its existing telephone network, is clearly designed to hasten the march towards that goal. Unlike mega-deals like the one discussed between AT&T and SBC, the Excel-Telco merger is seen as enhancing overall marketplace choices for the consumer. Excel and Telco Communications Group have entered into a definitive merger agreement. The transaction, valued at $1.2 billion, will create a company with $2 billion in revenue, 11 billion long distance minutes, 6.3 million customers, and 100,000 network miles of fiber-optic capacity.

The Global Marketplace

From around the corner to around the world—the growth potential for telecommunications knows few geographic boundaries. In the developed world, growth is being propelled by the trend toward privatization, deregulation, and technological advancements resulting in new products. In the developing world, the very fact that populous societies are poised and ready to enter the telecommunications age in a big way for the first time excites U.S. communications companies large and small, and Excel is no exception. The global telecommunications services market, already pegged at $600 billion in annual revenues, will surpass the $1 trillion mark early in the next century.

More than phone company profits are at stake. The companies and countries that lay claim to global telecommunications leadership will be those that lay claim to global economic leadership as well. In the Information Age, there can be no other way.

"For centuries, nations that could develop and apply new transportation technologies (Portugal in the fifteenth century, England in the nineteenth century) have become global leaders of their age," writes James Burnham of the Center for the Study of American Business at Washington University in St. Louis. In more recent times, Burnham explains, advances in oceangoing ships and marine engine design played an integral role, for example, in the rise of the Japanese steel industry to global dominance. "Thanks to innovations in transportation-related technology, the sizable costs of shipping heavy bulk materials fell dramatically," Burnham explains. "How else could they haul coal, iron ore and scrap from Australia, Brazil and the United States to Japan—and then ship finished steel back at large profits?"

The transportation mode of choice in the twenty-first century will be telecommunications, because the most important product to be shipped is and will be: information.

One dramatic outgrowth of the development of telecommunications is that service industry tasks can be performed anywhere. "Telecommunications provides the global transportation 'highway' for the work that is performed by Irish call center technicians, Indian software engineers and Jamaican data entry clerks," Burnham writes. All a nation or region needs to do to compete for those jobs and investments "is a decent telecommunications infrastructure, a work force with the necessary skills, and a business climate where individuals have the incentives to work, save and invest productively."

To take part, many countries, rich and poor, are embracing the principles of deregulation and competition that have triggered an explosion of growth in the U.S. market and have paved the way for companies like Excel:

o Since the United Kingdom's landmark sale of British Telecom in 1984, there have been nine European privitizations, mostly partial. Some have been wildly popular with investors. Spain's Telefonica de Espana, for example, is currently Europe's hottest telecom stock.

o This year alone, $30 billion worth of privitizations are underway, compared to just $4 billion in 1992.

o In 1997, the government of Israel has announced it will sell off a big chunk of its stake in the national phone company. Jordan and Turkey will do the same. Brazil plans to privatize its phone system in 1999.

Says the International Telecommunication Union's Tim Kelly: "I think that around the world, the argument against competition on the basis of a natural monopoly is pretty much dead."

"Look at the Philippines," Kelly continues. "Since competition was introduced, the number of new telephony subscribers each year has gone from between 10,000 and 20,000 a year to 200,000 a year." A top telecommunications official in Hong Kong notes: "There is a growing acceptance among policymakers and political leaders that increased competition and liberalization of telecommunications encourages infrastructure development, draws inbound investment, and assists in meeting universal service objectives."

Giant providers and entrepreneurial upstarts alike eagerly await the chance to fill the huge gaps in service that exist around the globe. Consider the following:

- For more than half of the world's 5.7 billion people, the primary means of communication is *not* the telephone.
- In richer countries, there are 50 lines for every 100 people.
- In low-income countries—those with a per capita gross domestic product of $725 or less—there were fewer than two phone lines for every 100 people. In some Southeast Asian countries, such as Laos, Myanmar, and Vietnam, there is less than one phone line per 100 people.
- In the world's most populous country, China, there are only about 3.3 phones per 100 people.
- Hong Kong's seven million inhabitants have more phones than do Indonesia's 200 million people.
- While the United States has more than 150 million phone lines servicing a 240 million

population, India has just 13 million for
930 million people.

The paucity of phone service in Asia will change dramatically overnight. As futurist John Naisbitt writes in
his recent book *Megatrends Asia:*

> The Asian continent now accounts for half the
> world's population. Within five years or less, more
> than half of these Asian households will be able to
> buy an array of consumer goods—refrigerators, tele-
> vision sets, washing machines, computers, cosmetics,
> etc. And as many as a half billion people will be what
> the West understands as middle class. That market
> is roughly the size of the United States and Europe
> combined.

Naisbitt identifies other developments that make
Asia a natural prospect market for U.S. telecommunications products and services:

- The number of Asians in poverty has decreased
  from 400 million to 180 million since the end
  of World War II, even while the population has
  increased another 400 million.
- The growing Asian middle class, not including
  Japan's, will have amassed $8 to $10 trillion in
  annual spending power shortly after the turn of
  the century.

○ Currently, more than 80 million mainland Chinese earn between $10,000 and $40,000 a year. In South Korea, 60 percent of those who describe themselves as middle class make over $60,000 a year. One million families in greater Bangkok, Thailand, earn over $10,000 annually.

These are not the kind of consumers who will remain telecommunications-deprived for very long!

Several years ago, while writing a book on business opportunities in Vietnam, I had a chance to view first-hand the stirring of a nascent Asian middle class in that developing country. The pace of economic change and the growth of consumer demand that I witnessed was staggering—and much of it was led by the availability of an array of communications technologies.

In the early 1990s, just as the country was beginning a transformation from a centrally planned socialist economy to one based on market incentives, I stayed at a premier hotel in the heart of Saigon, now called Ho Chi Minh City. The clerk at the front desk entered my name in a handwritten ledger. Bills were calculated on an abacus. There was a phone in my room, but it had no dial or keypad; it simply connected me to the hotel operator, and I had to compete for one of the two outside lines. Coming in from the airport, I rode in a vintage Peugeot that had been converted into a taxi. Mine was one of the only vehicles on the road that day that was not powered by foot.

On another trip just a year later, I rode in from the airport in a brand-new, air-conditioned Toyota taxicab. The streets were choked with new Honda motorcycles. Arriving at the same hotel, the clerk checked me in on her computer and totaled my bill on it too. My room had a Touch-Tone telephone that offered international direct dialing.

I also had the opportunity to visit a number of typical urban Vietnamese homes. Over the course of several trips I watched those homes load up on the latest gadgets and technologies in a breakneck fashion. One of the most sought-after prizes: a cellular phone. With wireless technology, many Vietnamese, as well as residents of other developing countries, are taking advantage of the chance to "leapfrog" technologies, bypassing the long, bureaucratic, and graft-ridden process of securing a land-based line.

Excel's top Representatives are no doubt tracking the growing popularity of the direct selling and network marketing approaches in regions such as Asia and Latin America. It's a natural fit, where the sales and business professions are lauded and where tapping vast networks of family and business connections are deeply rooted in the culture.

Information technology—and the sizable pool of Americans who trace their heritage back to these promising markets and thus possess valuable knowledge of culture, language, and contacts—make the network marketer's potential to expand his or her "territory" beyond the shores of America greater than ever before. In fact, the company whose name can be traced to the phrase American Way—Amway—now derives a greater portion of its sales from foreign markets than it does from the United States.

None of these exciting developments have escaped the watchful eye and creative imagination of Kenny Troutt. He has said that one of the reasons Excel is now moving towards its own switching and transmission network is to provide the capability to develop international markets. The first three switches are slated to be installed in New York, Dallas, and Los Angeles in 1997, chosen because of their position as gateways to the global economy. "But when we go into a country," Kenny says, as he warns competitors and thrills Excel Representatives, "we're not just doing it to get 2 or 3 percent of the market."

Electricity

Kenny Troutt delights in telling this story: As recently as a year ago, company lawyers advised him to remove from his speeches optimistic predictions that Excel would one day be able to go into the business of marketing electrical service the way it sells long-distance phone service. "It will never happen in our lifetime," they told him.

Today, it's just around the corner, and Excel plans to be ready.

"For the typical homeowner, electricity is a monopoly service: One either pays the power company or chops wood," writes Clyde Wayne Crews Jr., a fellow at the Competitive Enterprise Institute in Washington, D.C. "This will change if Congress deregulates the $208 billion electric industry to allow individual customers to choose among power companies. Economy-wide savings have been estimated at $24 billion annually."

Some states aren't waiting for Washington. On May 6, 1997, California regulators voted to allow power customers to go shopping for lower rates effective January 1, 1998. The prospect of winning a piece of the state's $20 billion market will trigger, predicts *Business Week,* "a modern gold rush" of companies seeking to buy power in bulk at discounted rates and resell it to consumers. "Under the new California rules," the magazine reports, "customers can secure lower cost power from inside or outside the state, paying their local utilities only for the costs of shipping to their home or business."

In all, eight states—Arizona, Massachusetts, New Hampshire, New York, Pennsylvania, Rhode Island, and Vermont, in addition to California—have adopted laws or regulatory orders providing for retail competition in electricity by next year or soon after.

Meanwhile, several bills have been introduced in Congress to break up regional monopolies that major utilities have enjoyed since the 1930s. Predicting a "legislative donnybrook," the *New York Times* reports that the issue will be one of the most closely watched and heavily lobbied issues before Congress in years.

"A high stakes battle is unfolding in Congress and across the country over legislation to give consumers the same choice in buying electricity that they now have in choosing airlines and long-distance telephone companies," the *Times* reported recently.

Excel will be well-positioned to once again cut through all the ad racket and nasty name-calling among competitors by appealing directly, on a one-to-one basis, with the most loyal base of customers a company can have: the family members, friends, and associates of the Independent Representatives who sell the services.

"Along with local phone service, electricity will be one of the most powerful products out there in the next five years," Kenny predicts. "I think we'll be in that market in less than two years."

Imagining the Future

"There are going to be products coming into our business that we don't even know of," Kenny tells the crowd of 1,500 Excel Representatives and their prospects in Los Angeles. "Together, we've gone out and changed the way business is done in the communications industry. We can do the same in the financial industry, in electricity, in insurance, and in the international marketplace. We've got an Internet plan coming. We might offer banking over the telephone, including loans and electronic transfer of funds. Let's call it FirstExcel!"

The ideas come fast and furious, and the crowd grows more excited by the minute. Every new product and every new service affords them an opportunity to achieve their financial goals that much faster. "Think what it would mean to all of us if we could increase our sales per customer from $30 a month to $200 a month."

"All you have to do is see the vision," Kenny likes to say. Tonight, they do. "The most important thing to understand about Kenny," Lisa Troutt has said, "is that when he says he's going to do something, you know for sure that he's going to do it."

Invoking that most valuable of lessons Mama Nadine taught him years ago, Kenny concludes by reminding the hopeful crowd, "My mother always told me, 'On the way to the stars, take as many people with you as you possibly can.'

"The rocket ship is taking off." Everyone is seeing the stars tonight.

AN INTERVIEW
WITH KENNY TROUTT

K enny Troutt never fails to recognize the team effort that has made his young company a success. Yet, so much about Excel is defined and driven by the ideas, strategies, and dreams of its founder and leader.

In June 1997, I had an opportunity to pose some questions to Kenny about Excel and his own life as one of America's most successful entrepreneurs.

If you had to sum up the key reasons for Excel's success, which factors would you cite?

Timing was a big factor. Excel was founded shortly after the breakup of AT&T, which placed us at the forefront of the explosive growth opportunities in telecommunications. Our choice to use network marketing as Excel's sole distribution method has been another key factor. Since the decision to go with network marketing, Excel's growth has been tremendous. Our success can also be attributed to our ability to provide competitively priced products and to offer our Independent Representatives what I believe is the greatest compensation plan in the industry. Beyond that, our success has been driven by the dreams of thousands of people all across the country. We're putting people in business for themselves and helping them achieve their personal and financial goals. Nothing has been a more powerful factor in our success than our ability to help them succeed individually.

You had no background in telecommunications, yet you have been able to build a billion-dollar telecommunications company from the ground up. What does this say about the telecommunications industry and about the American free enterprise system?

There's no question there are tremendous opportunities in telecommunications. It's one of the fastest-growing industries in the world. But I don't think you need to be a telecom expert to be successful. For me, it's all about developing a creative way to generate demand and then, obviously, to be able to satisfy that demand. And in my opinion, the American free enterprise system is still the greatest vehicle in the world for allowing that to happen. It's a system that still rewards hard work and good ideas.

While your business career has been a great success, you have had some setbacks along the way. What have you learned from the setbacks and the mistakes? What advice do you have to offer people just starting out in business when things don't always go their way?

Never lose sight of why you're doing what you're doing. You have to take a setback and look for the positives, and there are always some positives. Setbacks test your ability as a leader, and getting past them and moving forward makes you a better one. The people who succeed are the ones who never stop reaching for their dreams, the ones who never forget why they started in the first place.

Why do you think so many Americans are looking to the possibilities of starting their own business? Do you think this is a major, lasting trend in our society?

Most people, given the opportunity, want to be in business for themselves. I don't think that's a trend, that's just free enterprise. Network marketing, on the other hand, is a trend that I believe will continue to gain in popularity, because it provides an alternative to the traditional start-up business that is less costly and in many cases offers greater income potential.

What are some things government can do, in Washington or in each state, to make the climate more attractive for entrepreneurs like you and your Excel Reps?

Personally, I'd like to see the state governments become more actively involved in identifying and regulating

211

questionable business practices operating under the guise of legitimate network marketing companies.

What do you consider the three or four most important developments on the horizon in telecommunications, in business, and in society that are really going to shape the future of Excel?

First, I believe that network marketing will continue to gain in popularity in the business sector as many companies begin to explore it as an additional, cost-effective vehicle for the distribution of their products and services. Second, it will grow in the private sector as more and more people leave the confines of corporate America to start their own home-based business, providing them with more flexibility and greater income. Consequently, the exciting thing about this trend for Excel is that all of these new home-business owners will need communications services. By providing competitively priced bundles of communications products, including local and long-distance phone service, PCS, Internet access, and so on, I expect our IRs to attract many of them as Excel customers. It's a win-win situation.

Excel was established as a switchless reseller. With so much success from that approach, why are you taking steps to own your own facilities?

We still have contracts with WorldCom, MCI, IXC, and Frontier to handle Excel traffic. As our business continues to grow, having our own network adds more capacity and enables greater cost savings, which makes Excel more competitive, to help us better meet our customers' needs.

In June 1997, Excel entered a definitive agreement to acquire Telco Communications Group. What does the decision to acquire Telco mean to Excel Representatives?

The Telco acquisition gives us a competitive edge in the commercial and international markets even faster than we had originally planned. Telco's network gives us a platform for enhanced products and service in both these areas, and it saves us the time and expense of starting from scratch. Strategically, I believe it's a tremendous move for Excel.

Should Excel Reps be concerned that Telco has its own in-house sales force?

Not at all. Every decision I make as the CEO of Excel Communications, I make with our Independent Representatives in mind. The Telco acquisition is no exception. Telco's in-house sales force of about 300 people will be a valuable resource that will complement our IRs as they approach larger business accounts.

When can we expect to see Excel's first moves into foreign markets? Which markets or regions are you eyeing first? What will be the general approach to entering a foreign market?

We are researching the possibilities right now and are confident that entering the international markets will provide a tremendous growth opportunity for Excel and for our IRs. A number of multilevel companies have entered those markets and have been highly successful. Most likely, our first international markets will be Canada, Mexico, United Kingdom, Australia, and New Zealand, to name a few.

What are Excel's plans for playing in the local telephone sweepstakes? Can you make inroads there, given the intense competition?

I hope to introduce local service into the Excel product mix—at least on a limited basis—by the end of 1997. It's an important part of our strategic plan and one I believe will have a tremendous impact on the company. As far as competition in that marketplace is concerned, I feel that as long as our Independent Representatives have an incentive to go back to their existing customers, we can compete favorably. Those customers already know us. It shouldn't be a difficult sale.

You've spoken about the potential of selling electricity. Where does that stand? Is electricity a good fit for a communications company?

That's an industry that will also offer some tremendous opportunities, although it will be several years before we move in that direction. I do think it's a great fit for Excel, because it's another consumable product that we can introduce to our customer base.

As you expand and grow the company, moving it into new directions, will the role of the Independent Representatives change?

I don't see their role changing, although they may be even busier. Excel will continue to provide them with new products and services they can sell to their warm markets. They will always be the driving force behind our growth and success.

Describe what you would like Excel to look like in 20 years.

Excel will be a global communications company, offering a large variety of products and services, using in every country in the world the same marketing concept we use today. Excel has changed the lives of many people in the United States, and I would like people all over the world to have that same opportunity.

In June 1997, Excel named Jack McLaine as president and chief operating officer. What does this mean for Excel and how will it impact your role as chief executive officer?

As president and COO, Jack is responsible for the development of finance, technology, and legal and administrative functions as well as all back-office operations and strategic business development. In a word, Jack will handle the day-to-day operations of the company and keep me informed of any issues that require special attention. As CEO and chairman of the board, I will now be able to spend more time focusing on the marketing plan and future products—providing even more opportunities for our Independent Representatives.

Conclusion

1. Is your income growing as fast as you'd like and does it have the potential to grow in the future?
2. In the event of retirement, the loss of a job, or an unexpected catastrophic expense, do you have enough savings that would permit you to maintain your current lifestyle?
3. Do you feel that you're in control of your daily schedule?
4. Do you have enough time to spend with your spouse and your children?
5. Will you be content with relying on the government in Washington, D.C., to take care of you and provide for your needs, or are you the kind of person who wants to stand on your own?
6. Have you ever wanted to be your own boss?
7. Do you believe that the telecommunications industry will continue to grow for years to come?
8. Do you think you know a few close friends or family members who, if you asked them, would become your long distance customers—especially if it saved them money and didn't change the way they made their calls?

9. Do you get personal satisfaction from helping others and from surrounding yourself with interesting and successful people?

10. Do you strongly believe that in America the future can always be better than the past for those willing to work hard, take a chance, and try something new?

If you've answered these questions the way most of us have and do, then you're ready to jump aboard Kenny Troutt's "rocket ship to the stars." And in so doing, you can promote yourself to the ranks of those visionary Americans who, rather than being overwhelmed by the change, help shape it, lead it, and ride it into the future.

How can such change be defined? What are the most important trends for you to watch, manage, and jump in front of?

○ The global telecommunications industry, operating in a deregulated environment, will be the most powerful and lucrative industry during the opening decades of the new millennium. It will be marked by explosive growth, creating hundreds of new billionaires and tens of thousands of new millionaires in our lifetimes.

○ The rise of the self-employed will continue, as Americans hasten their march away from the corporate world to start their own businesses.

The self-employed, already accounting for a share of population equal to that of the unionized workforce, will constitute a growing political and social force in our society, demanding government policies that encourage rather than punish individual initiative.

○ Network marketing will continue to gain acceptance and potency in the business world and consumer marketplace. Low-cost technology will make starting these businesses easier than ever before, with greater odds for success than ever before. The transformation of network marketing from a product-based to a service-based industry will vastly increase the growth of the industry and attract droves of new practitioners from the ranks of the most highly skilled professions.

○ The security once offered by big government and big companies will continue to crumble. Faced with burdens of an aging population, the government will continue to scale back social safety net programs, leaving millions of Americans in the lurch. Intense global competition will force big companies, even in the face of a booming economy, to engage in almost continual rounds of downsizing, automation, and mergers—all of which may be good for the company but will spell uncertainty and risk for employees. The inability of government and the traditional business world to provide the level of security and opportunity Americans once enjoyed will propel many into the ranks of small-business owners.

○ A crisis in values—the breakdown of the family, growing drug use among youth, the decline of the education system, the threat of violent crime, the shunning of personal responsibility, and the disintegration of community spirit—will unleash a powerful political, social, and cultural movement aimed at restoring those values. This movement will be based on the reaffirmation of self-reliance, individual initiative, full-time parenting, and educational choice. It will inspire many to change careers and rearrange personal priorities. It will reaffirm the ethic of a compassionate capitalism in which people succeed by helping others succeed. And it will return the entrepreneur, who works hard, dreams big, and risks all, to a place of high honor in our country.

Index

A

Adler, Jordan, 98–99

Amway, xvi, 40

AT&T, xi, 2, 11, 18, 31, 106, 148, 194–196, 209

    break-up of, 12–15

    current market position, 15–17

B

Beck, Greg and Carolyn, 47–48

Bell, Alexander Graham, 5–8, 24

Bowditch, Larry and Lucille, 86–89

Brake, Rick and Cindy, 99–100

breakdown of the American family, 118–124

C

Casner, Bill and Susan, 31, 33–34, 46

Cheatham, Larry and Bonnie, 124

Cross, Bob and Linda, 145–146

D

Davis, Randy and Melissa, 69, 115–118, 130

Dick, Jimmy, 167–168

Dickson, Don, 145

Direct Selling Assn., 58, 165, 177

E

Eckart, Philip, 160–161

economic insecurity, 92–97

Edison, Thomas, 8

electricity deregulation,
204–206

Excel Communications, Inc.

accomplishments of,
186–187

appeal to IRs, 20–22

and the Better Business
Bureau, 171–172

business strategy of,
17–19

customer services and
products, 19–20,
189–207

growth of, 4

initial public offering
(IPO), 22–23,
25–26

merger with Telco, xiv-xv,
197, 213

recognition of top
performers, 68–69

"Stairway to Success,"
64–68

F

Federal Communications
Commission (FCC),
11, 12, 13, 171, 177,
191

Friedman, Loren and Vicki,
125–127

Funk, Dave and Ellen,
135–137

G

Gergen, John and Alice, 127

Gilmore, Kenny and Linda,
100–101

Greene, Harold, 14, 15

H

Hallmark, Daryl and Betty,
142–143

Hankins, Vivian, 47–48

Head, Ron and Judy, 146–147

Hillis, Hugh and Denise,
148–150

Hinson, Beth, 101–102

Hintze, Cindy, 102–103

Hintze, Pat, 2, 74, 102–103,
130

Hoover, Chuck and Sandra,
85–86

Hundt, Reed, 192–193

J

Jennings, David and Karen,
103–105

Johnson, Kern, 87
Jones, John and Patrice,
    105–106

K

Kelly-Smith, Meg, 7, 69,
    128–130
Kirkland, Ronny, 147–148,
    149

L

Lammons, Mike and Barbara,
    69, 78–83
Lemons, Lee, 87, 88, 110–111
Lemons, Rhonda, 110–111

M

Martignon, Dan and Linda,
    34–35
MCI, 2, 13, 18, 148, 166,
    170, 212
McLaine, Jack, xv, 23–24, 32,
    41, 184, 215–216
Medicare, 137, 139–140, 141
Mims, Phil and Lucie,
    132–133

N

Ness, Susan, 193

network marketing (multi-
    level marketing)
    advantages of, 58–59
    as compared to pyramid
        schemes, 161–163
    growth of, 58
Noland, Russ and Mary, 69,
    106–107

O-P

Orberson, Paul, 38, 40, 69,
    75–77, 85, 180
paging, 189–190
Parrill, Fred and Charlotte,
    31, 34, 47
Pentecost, Mark and Cindy,
    130–132
Phibbs, Glen and Charlene,
    150–151
Pine, Kevin and Doreen,
    108–109
Pospichal, Scott and Brenda,
    83–84

R-S

Ricketts, Rick and Brenda,
    77–78
Schulz, Colleen, 74
Schulz, Steve, 2, 3, 71, 74

Scott, J. R. and Betty,
109–110
Shaklee, 17
Smith, Jay, 128–130
Smith, Sarah, 53, 155–157
Smith, Steve, xv, 24, 32, 41,
63–64, 68, 76, 77,
184
involvement in Excel,
52–53, 55–56,
159–160, 185–186
personal background,
50–52
Social Security, 137,
138–139, 140, 141
Sprint, 3, 18, 148, 166

T
Telco Communications
Group, xiv, 4, 23, 32,
196, 213
Telecommunications Act of
1996, 192–196
Telecommunications Resellers
Assn., 170
Telecommunications
services
demands for, 9–11

regulation of, 11–17
world growth of,
197–202
Telephone
growth of, 8–11
invention of, 5–9
Thomas, Al, 69, 111–114,
185
Thompson, Michael,
107–108
Torsey, Bob and Lois, 72–74
Triplett, LaDonna, 143–144
Troutt, Kenny, xi, xiii, xiv, xv,
4, 23, 24, 25, 26, 68,
73, 76, 77, 80, 104,
126, 133, 143, 147,
148, 157, 165, 170,
180, 184, 186, 187,
188, 189, 196, 204,
206
awards of, 42
childhood, 26–28
early business ventures,
28–32
idea for Excel, 32
interview with, 209–216
leadership abilities,
45–46

marriage to Lisa Troutt, 36
starting Excel, 32–36
Troutt, Grant Michael, 37
Troutt, Lisa, 26, 207
    at Excelebration 1996,
        38–39, 41
    marriage to Kenny, 36–37
Troutt, Preston Allen, 37

W
Walker, Steve and Roberta, 125
Watson, Thomas A., 6, 7, 24
Wells, Phillip, 84–85
wireless phones, 190–192
Witt, Barbara, 151–152
Wittmann, Pete, 28, 29, 30,
        31, 32, 33, 35–36